OBLI\
BUT TRUE

JEAN KELFORD

A BLACKIE & CO PUBLISHERS PAPERBACK

c Copyright 2002
Jean Kelford

The right of Jean Kelford to be identified as the author of this work has been asserted by her in accordance with the Copyright, Designs and Patents Act 1988

First Published in 2002

A CIP catalogue record for this title is available from the British Library

ISBN   1 903138 54 X

Blackie & Co Publishers Ltd
107-111 Fleet Street
LONDON EC4A 2AB

ACKNOWLEDGEMENTS

My heartfelt and everlasting thanks go to my husband Mike, without whom I could not help people through my work with Spirit. My children, stepchildren, grandchildren, Mum, Dad, and all other members of my family and friends, both here and in Spirit. Especially friends such as Laureece, Annie, Sue, TES, Polly, Caroline, Carol, Fred, Margaret and Hugh.

It is thanks to the above people that both my life, and this book have been possible.

I would also like to pay special tribute to Doris Stokes, for all the help and inspiration she has given to us whilst working with Spirit. To my stepdaughter Jenny, who passed to the Spirit side of life on Saturday, August 9th, 1997. She is wholly responsible for me writing the poems which are in this book, and we love her dearly. To Denise and Claire, for all their inspiration, both here and from Spirit. They, like many others, work on from the Spirit side of life, and I ask everyone to try and do the same, whilst still here, and not to wait until you pass to Spirit. Because this helps those in Spirit, to help us. My love and blessings go to you all.

Many thanks go to James Childs, who designed the cover, based on the design by Jean and Mike Kelford.

Warmest Regards

Jean

FOREWORD

I decided to write this book because so many people have asked me to. It is not intended to be an all-encompassing account of my life with all its spiritual episodes – purely because there's too much material for one volume. It is, rather, a collection of some of my more significant experiences so far.

Growing up, for me, was a catalogue of strange occurrences and visions whose significance I didn't understand until later. Of course, anyone would be confused by such experiences – and for a child they're bound to be particularly bewildering. Perhaps if I'd been a less innocent child I'd have understood more. Probably not – I'm inclined to believe that things only happen when the time is right. I read somewhere that there's no such thing as coincidence – that it's just God having a quiet word with you. I think the same can be said for the Spirit world – its inhabitants sometimes talk to us in the symbolism of coincidence as a means of making us understand what might otherwise be beyond us.

I appreciate that the visions I've experienced throughout my life and which are familiar to me will be alien to those who have never witnessed such things – so I shall try to explain them.

I still remember vividly my first vision as an adult. I was walking down our street when suddenly a picture appeared in front of me. It was crystal clear, full colour and just like a television – except that it was circular. The 'programme' showing was of some laughing children sitting on a red carpet, playing Pass-The-Parcel. One child's smile shrivelled to a quivering frown and her laughter choked, stalled and turned to tears as she cried, 'It's my turn to open it!' The girl next to her had snatched the parcel from her so that she missed her turn.

I was puzzled to say the least. Nevertheless this same scene played itself out to me on numerous occasions until, a short time

1

afterwards, I ordered a new carpet. For some reason, though, the shop delivered the wrong one – but we decided to keep it anyway because it was exactly the colour and pattern of the one in my recurring vision! When my daughter's birthday came around the scene was instantly familiar – all the children sitting on the carpet, playing Pass-The-Parcel. It wasn't just familiar – events were identical!

Many more visions followed – some about imminent world events, which would then appear on the news and others about what was to happen to people close to me. My sister, Hazel (more of whom later), always liked to hear about the visions so that she could look out for them actually happening.

One morning I had a vision of my son lying on his back by a wall; arms outstretched, palms upward. Whether he was dead or unconscious I did not know – but I could see a sewing needle piercing his wrist. Needless to say Hazel (she was staying with me at the time) and I were very worried. Later that day my son's school phoned to say he'd had an accident. Riding his friend's bike, he'd hit a wooden stump and been flung over the handlebars. They'd found him lying unconscious in precisely the position I had foreseen. What's more, he had to have stitches in his wrist!

Another time, whilst Hazel was staying with me, I had a vision of her with bright orange hair. She laughed hysterically when I told her, assuring me that this was one vision that definitely wouldn't come true! The following week she asked my opinion of a local hairdresser – because her hair was bleached blonde and the roots needed doing. I said I didn't know what they were like and she went ahead and booked an appointment later that week. After her appointment she came home with bright orange hair. The bleaching had gone horribly wrong!

These are just three examples of many strange moments – but the more you develop and the more you know, the easier these things are to understand and cope with.

In my opinion I'm one of the lucky ones because strong psychic ability and mediumship are present in both sides of my family – which means I got a double dose of psychic power. Of course, that doesn't mean I don't understand how difficult it can be for others.

I hope that this book at least begins to make people aware how ordinary mediums are. I'd also hope that the exercises in later chapters will help those of you who want to develop to go forward – and that they will be of interest to those who don't wish to take it any further.

These exercises can also help people to relax – thereby making life easier to handle. Understanding our spiritual side does help us to understand ourselves because, after all, we too are spirits.

CHAPTER 1

Beginnings

At 9 AM on the morning of August 22nd, 1952, I put in my first appearance in this world. My mother says that she remembers still being on rations – and that once a month they received extra sugar. I was born on the day that the extra sugar arrived. I wasn't aware of this until recently, yet I've always had a strong interest in sugar and used to get books from the library on the cultivation of sugar cane.

My mum would sit at the large wooden table in our dining room, where there'd be a tray of tea things and, often, a little spilt sugar. She used to crack the granules with her nail, which always fascinated me. Strangely enough, I don't have a particularly sweet tooth – in fact I don't drink sugary drinks at all.

My point is that we are psychically drawn to certain things in life for many reasons. In this case, sugar had a direct link to my birth, making it the entry into this world of my Guardian Angel – who would guard and protect me throughout my life.

I joke with Mum that I was sweetness itself and that this was the real reason for my affinity – but I'm sure you'd agree that the first explanation is more likely.

I was the third child and third daughter. My parents would go on to have nine children, five of whom were girls and four boys.

I realise now that they all could be mediums. However, growing up in a busy family with a hectic life I wasn't aware that some of the people with whom I regularly conversed were actually dead and that I was talking with the spirit world!

I can't claim to remember the day I was born – but I say without hesitation that I was aware of the spirit world from the very beginning of my life in this one. I was so sure of this that I grew up believing that everyone shared my awareness and knowledge of these people with whom I held conversations daily. This, of course, included the animal kingdom.

If asked to reminisce about my childhood, again I would have quite a mixture of stories that most would think unusual. My first memory – which I can now relate to the spirit world – was when I was four. My sister, Chris – affectionately known to my Dad as 'Crispo' – is thirteen months older than me. As children, we did most things together – something of which I was very proud. However, on this occasion I'd have been happy not to have joined her!

She had fallen ill with pneumonia, having suffered with a bad chest all her life, and had been taken to hospital. I missed her sorely until, unfortunately, I too came down with pneumonia and joined her in hospital. I clearly remember being carried down the hospital corridor by the ambulance-man. All I could see were people in beds with red blankets over them. Although red was the standard colour for hospital blankets in those days, they scared me and made me cry. Suddenly, a lady in a uniform and a large hat came up behind us. She stroked my hair and said, gently, 'Don't cry Jean. I'm here with you.'

I wasn't sure why, but I was fascinated by the realisation that I knew that I was safe with this woman. I was put in the bed next to my sister's, which made me feel better instantly. We always laughed a lot when we were together and this time was no exception. Although she'd been more poorly than I, she went home first because she'd gone into hospital a few days earlier. I was upset because I wanted to go home too – or of course for Chris to stay. The lady in the funny hat appeared again and tried to comfort me – to which I replied that I'd be all right if only Chris could stay for one more day. Strangely enough, the ambulance which was due to collect her didn't turn up, which meant that Chris had to undress again and stay until the next day. Selfish as it may seem, I was really pleased!

This lady was to appear many times throughout my life – and she still does. It turns out that she was a nurse many years ago and she looks after me and those close to me whenever we are worried or unwell. My children too came to know her very well, since all three are lucky enough to see the spirit world just as I do. They all have memories of seeing her walking up and down in their bedrooms whenever they were unwell as children. With this in mind, I often wonder whether she deliberately delayed that ambulance in order to help me – after all, my sister didn't mind being there as long as I was there too.

Strange as it may seem, most of my memories include the spirit world in some way. Although many members of my immediate family are afraid of the dark, I never shared their fear. This is because, as far back as I can remember, there has been a man close by whom I know very well and trust implicitly. Ever since I was able to go to the bathroom alone I've seen him on the stairs – always there to reassure me and protect me from harm.

As time went by I would come to know this man very well – in fact it's mainly because of him that I'm a medium today. He is my Guardian Angel; my main guide from the spirit world. As this book progresses I'll be referring to him from time to time – probably as 'the man on the stairs' at first, then later by his name.

Another companion from my infant years was a young girl called Amy who used to talk with me often, mostly about things which didn't make sense at the time, or which it didn't seem possible that she could know. She was - and is – a very nice young lady but, to my surprise, almost everyone else was oblivious to her presence. She asked me not to tell anyone that we played and talked together – so I didn't tell a soul, apart from dropping the occasional hint to Chris. This was unusual. I normally told her everything and vice versa. Of course, now that we're grown-up, I realise that she probably knew anyway.

As children, we spent many happy hours looking out of the bedroom window in the evenings. We'd stare up at the sky, watching the clouds float by and taking turns to describe the shapes we saw and what they meant to us. Spirit guides (I now know that's what Amy is) come in very handy when you need to know what the clouds are saying to you. I suppose I was an unusual child in lots of ways. For example, my family remembers my wearing my duffel coat, hood and all, in the middle of summer. Everyone else was saying how hot it was while I was very definitely cold.

It wasn't until many years later that I realised why Amy had asked me to keep her visits secret. It was because not everyone can see her, hear her or even sense her presence. One of Amy's jobs in the spirit world is to exchange fear, vulnerability and loneliness for peace, laughter and love. Having realised this, I once asked why I became extremely cold whenever she was around. It didn't, after all, seem to fit with the notions of peace, laughter and love! She laughed, saying:

'It's only because I've been in the spirit world for many years – and that means we come in on a cold vibration. This is because the longer we are in the spirit world, the more planes of existence we progress through – so we have further to travel to reach you. Because we occupy the same space as you, but on a much higher wavelength, the speed with which we join you brings about a frisson of cold air. Feeling this cold from the spirit world means excessive love!

You see I'm not really still a little girl. The age at which you see me is my age when I passed to the spirit world. Although I'm now grown-up, I prefer to be a little girl – so I'm allowed to be just that. I should explain that once you've passed over from your world to mine, time is no longer of importance. The most important thing is love. It is, after all, the vibration of love that allows us to cross over from where we exist now to the existence we once knew as life.'

It was at this point that my curiosity really got the better of me. Questions were popping into my head at a great rate of knots. I answered,

'All right, if you say it's the vibration of love that allows us to communicate with one another, I believe you. But what is this vibration of love?'

At that moment, Amy disappeared. This wasn't unusual for her – in fact I'd become used to her sudden departures without knowing why they happened. This time, though, I was caught by surprise but before I had time to reflect, I was overwhelmed by a feeling of perfect peace; a feeling so real that I could almost touch it; a silence you could almost hear. There in front of me stood someone else I'd got to know well.

He's a gentleman from Russia, standing almost seven feet tall and wearing a top hat. His name, I'm told, is Izeakial Ramminskicorsicoff and he's my Guardian Angel or main guide. This means he's around whenever I need help or direction – as I surely did right then! He put his right hand in front of his face, arm outstretched, palm towards me in a 'stop' gesture. 'Wait. Slow down my child. I will explain,' he said. Having known him all my life I knew not to be impatient. He would answer my as-yet-unvoiced questions in his own time. Lowering his hand, he half-smiled and said:

'The answer you're waiting for is a simple one. The word love is a word with which everyone is familiar. We all love someone or

8

something at some time during our lives – even if it is ourselves. Do you understand?'

Although moments before I'd had lots of things to say, I suddenly couldn't think of one. So I was silent. He continued as though there had been no interruption:

'The word love is spelled: L, O, V, E. The meanings of those four letters are: "Light of Vibration Eternity". Do you understand, my child?'

I can't put into words how I felt at that moment but I can say that I now know what love means.

You may find it strange that I talk to this most unusual man who spoke so differently from the way we now accept as the norm. What you need to bear in mind, though, is the fact that he's been around for as long as I can remember, sitting on the stairs while I sleep. I usually have a chat with him if I go to the bathroom during the night. This has been part of my life wherever I've lived – so it's completely natural to me. Often, after I've been in bed for about ten minutes I hear his footsteps crossing the landing outside my bedroom. Then the door handle goes down and the door opens suddenly. This would be scary stuff for those who don't understand the spirit world – but not for me. As I've said before, it's completely natural to me.

Throughout my childhood the fact that these people were dead escaped me – probably a good thing too because it might have made me afraid of the unknown like so many others. In my experience, people aren't really afraid of the spirit world as such – more of the unknown factor we call 'dying'. Death, after all, is a word like any other until you add to it the knowledge that we all die – which naturally leads to the question on most people's lips:

'What is death?'

And the next question:

'What happens to us when we die?'

Or:

'Where do we go when we die?'

Of course, all this is for the people curious enough to accept that there really is something else. It is sometimes easier to dismiss the unknown than to accept that there might be something without being sure what it is. I can't tell you why as a child I didn't suspect the reality of things – but I can say how proud and pleased I am that this knowledge came to me naturally, for my own guidance and to help many others along the way.

If you're curious and open-minded, you've taken the first step towards knowing that the spirit world exists and that its inhabitants can and do communicate with the living.

I'd like to ask readers to bear in mind what's made them decide to read this book. For some it may be purely the fact that they know me and are naturally interested in reading what I have to say. For others, it will be a keen interest in anything to do with the spirit world; a thirst for knowledge about a subject that's surrounded with so much controversy and is therefore fascinating. There will be many reasons for reading this book but I put it to you that since you're reading it, you're curious. So you've taken the first step. The next is to read on with an open mind!

CHAPTER 2

Innocence

The innocence of children makes it easier for Spirits to get in touch. Sceptics might say that this is because children are gullible. It's an understandable conclusion when you consider my own incomprehension of the people I was in touch with as a child. On the other hand, perhaps it's just that children haven't yet learned to blinker themselves like adults. After all, their education in life can only come from the people around them.

Growing up in a large family (four sisters and four brothers, one of whom is in the Spirit world), I remember listening with interest to my parents' spiritual experiences. But I was never afraid – in fact I've always found it hard to understand people's fear of the dark. Personally, I've always known I was safe.

If Chris wasn't around, I'd happily chat and play with Amy without giving a moment's thought to where she lived; where she came from. Call it gullibility or innocence – but any way you look at it, it's acceptance! I accepted these other people as part of my life and my already large family. And I loved them as much too!

I'm telling you all this because I'd like my more sceptical readers to give me the benefit of the doubt – and to believe me when I say that Spirits really do exist. The rest of you have already taken the first step – which is accepting the possibility that we live on and come back to communicate with our loved ones. It means you're curious; it means you're open-minded.

Whilst talking to me, Amy would go to great lengths to explain how she had died because of a fire, which made her drown. Of course this didn't make any sense at all – until you hear the whole story. Having been badly burnt when a fire broke out in the barn-like shack her family called home, Amy received virtually no treatment because her family couldn't afford it – there being no National Health Service in those days. Both of her parents died within eighteen months of each other in separate incidents while Amy was very young – her father in an accident at the sawmill where he worked when she was almost four and her mother while giving birth to Amy's brother Charles.

Amy was adopted by Jack and Mary Randell – not because they liked children – they evidently did not – but because in order to use her as unpaid domestic labour. Worse still, Mary called Amy by her second name, Sarah, claiming that she preferred it. Mary knew that the name reminded Amy of her mother and was upsetting to her but used it regardless as a way of making Amy toe the line and do as she was told. I, however, shall use her proper name throughout this book.

Amy's father, Fred Burke, had been an amiable enough man but not very clever and he had his meagre means which were not enough to provide for his children after his death. Amy's arms, right leg and torso were severely scarred by the fire. These should have been treated continuously and above all kept dry if they were to heal well. Unfortunately, her washing duties meant that the wounds were almost constantly wet and never had a chance to heal. It was this that led to her fate.

Made to wash the family's clothes in a giant barrel of water in the back yard, she would clamber up onto a concrete boulder to reach far enough into the tub. One day she dropped the soap into tub and, afraid to tell Mary, she stretched down in an effort to reach it. Over-reaching herself, her scarred flesh being too stiff to manoeuvre easily, toppled into the barrel. Her rigid limbs could not find purchase on the barrel; she struggled, panicked and, tragically, drowned.

For me, going to school was a happy experience. I loved school and particularly enjoyed being in the Infants because it was time for myself. If that sounds strange, bear in mind that you don't get any time alone in a large family like mine – everyone has to do their bit. The extensive family has many good points – for instance, you learn how to do housework, look after babies and young children, cook, wash up and do the shopping at quite a young age, which is all good preparation for adult life. You also learn to share your possessions and your time – but sometimes it would have been nice to have some peace and quiet; a bit of space in which to do your own thing. Even whilst doing your homework you had to learn to put up with the constant noise and constant interruptions. Mind you, this does teach you to concentrate on more than one thing at a time – sometimes even listening to and responding to two conversations at the same time! When it comes to communicating with the spirit world this helps a lot because it involves listening and answering simultaneously. Sometimes you also have to listen to the person for whom the message is intended while other spirit people are vying for your attention. – which is quite a feat of concentration!

So you see my upbringing has been a great help. Generally, people aren't aware that television, radio and computers prevent us making full use of our senses. Actually, when I was young I didn't watch much television. Admittedly we didn't have one until I was older. But even when we acquired one I'd always be told to make a cup of tea as the programme was about to start. By the time I'd made tea for everyone, the programme would be halfway through so that it was hard to get interested. Instead, I'd settle down on the floor behind my dad's armchair and chat with Amy. I quickly learnt that I didn't need to speak out loud for her to hear me and we conversed in silence so that I wouldn't get shouted at for making a noise. Even if the programme wasn't well under way by the time I'd made tea, there were never any seats left. But behind my dad was the family's organ – and its cushioned foot-pedals served as my pillows as I lay on the floor. If we were in the back room I'd sit under the large wooden kitchen table out of the way in the hope that someone else would get collared for whatever job was at hand and I could get on with my homework.

Junior school was a different story because that's when I began to be bullied. This was partly because I came from such a large family and my clothes were usually my sisters' or my mum's friends' daughters' hand-me-downs. It was also partly because I was too gentle to retaliate and also very shy – which made me an easy target. Bullies tend to go for shy people because they know they'll meet little resistance. I did have a group of close friends who'd stand up for me and I'm sure they'd be surprised to see me these days happily addressing large congregations in my work as a medium!

Once I was in bed at night I could talk to the people of whom everyone else seemed oblivious. I had to sleep with the lights on because my two older sisters, with whom I shared a room, were afraid of the dark. But I'd put my head under the blankets to block out every last bit of light before speaking to Izeakial. Actually I never dared to use his first name – he said it showed lack of respect. Instead I still address him as Mr Ramminskicorsicoff or, mostly, as 'Sir'. For the rest of this book, though, I shall call him Izeakial because it's shorter – and I'm sure he won't mind in the circumstances.

Our talks were very informative and since my family didn't know the source of my new-found knowledge, they thought I dreamed it or simply made it up. This always puzzled me. I just couldn't understand why they couldn't see the people I could see. What did Dad mean when he said that I had an over-active imagination? This is how I got into the habit of talking to my guides for at least ten minutes every night before going to sleep and for another ten minutes on waking each morning. I'd recommend this to anyone who wants to get used to communicating with the spirit world. Sometimes they show you very detailed information about all sorts of things, which can be a bit scary until you get used to it. Mostly, though, it is fascinating.

When I was nine, my uncle died. He'd spent some time in a wheelchair, having suffered from shell-shock since the war – although I feel that the family was never quite sure what was the matter with him. It was my first experience of someone close to me dying. I cried although I hadn't known him very well – perhaps it was just the awareness of death that upset me.

Just before my tenth birthday my grandmother on my dad's side passed to the spirit world. This time, though, I couldn't cry – and felt bad about it for a long time because I'd known her very well. Having given this a great deal of thought, I feel sure that my lack of tears was because I was afraid of her. My grandmother was very strong-minded and strict and, when in her company, you didn't dare move a muscle without her permission.

Actually it was while visiting her that I learnt to astral travel. She'd go to the kitchen, leaving us sitting in the parlour. As she did so she'd tell us not to move because she had eyes in the back of her head and she'd see us if we did. Because she always seemed to know everything, even when she wasn't looking, we completely believed her. I used to say the same thing to my children as they grew up – I'd tell them off and they'd ask, 'how did you know that…You had your back to us,' to which I'd reply that I had eyes in the back of my head. The truth was that I used to come out of my body to see what they were up to!

I now realise that perhaps my grandmother was doing the same thing. Mind you, her manner was so sharp that we'd never dare to look for the eyes in the back of her head – we just took her word for it. Moving around in her presence was out of the question but I found that I could slip out of my body and go into the kitchen without her knowing I'd even moved. My sisters never caught on because we weren't allowed to talk – so they could hardly notice my absence.

My grandmother was High Church of England by religion but would often say that she didn't believe in life after death. However, one evening she suddenly screamed and my Dad and his brother ran downstairs to find her by the front parlour door. She told them she'd seen a man go into the room and described him in great detail. As the men were about to investigate, she stopped them, telling them to fetch a poker for protection. This they did, then entered the room, only to find it empty! There were locks on the windows and no other doors – no possible escape route. When told there was no one there, Grandmother said she must have imagined the whole thing. This seemed unlikely given that she'd described the man so clearly. Having said that she didn't believe in the spirit world, she obviously wasn't about to consider that as a possible explanation!

It was at this time of life that I found myself thinking about death – although I still had no idea that I'd been communicating with the dead for most, if not all, of my life. Growing up was a confusing time for me. I spent a lot of time dressing up as various elderly people, which made my friends and family laugh. They just thought it was me being me – a bit of a comedian with a good sense of humour. Yet really I was trying in earnest to portray the various people who'd spoken to me on a given day, or perhaps the previous night.

If only I had realised that the spirit world was there helping. I'm sure that if I had I would have understood who they were much sooner. My brothers, Keith and Kenneth, who were five and seven years younger than me respectively, were very close. While I babysat them for my mum and dad, I used to entertain them with 'magic' tricks, with the help of my psychic powers. Of course it wasn't magic at all but it kept them quiet for hours at a time. Keith would squeal with delight and shout, 'Do it again, Jean. Show us some more magic! Tell her Ken!' It was wonderful to watch the pair of them getting so excited – even though I knew that I wasn't moving those marbles around by sleight of hand or the kind of magic they had in mind.

I was about twelve when death came close again. One of my four close schoolfriends used to bring her six-year-old sister with her when she came to play at our house. Sadly, the younger sister suffered from a hole in the heart and died suddenly. My friend was never quite the same again – all the fun had gone out of her. I was deeply affected – both on behalf of my friend and of her sister, who had become a friend too. I found it hard to understand how someone just half my age could possibly die. From that day on I worried about dying – probably because I didn't understand, which is part of my reason for writing this book: to help people to understand that there is no death.

Around this time the spirits grew much stronger in the way that they communicated with me. I remember quite clearly telling my mum about a gorilla that must have escaped from a local zoo. She laughed but to me it was very real and I was very careful on the way home from school in case it leapt out of the bushes at me. I now realise that we all have an animal spirit with us for protection and that mine is a silverback gorilla of which I have no reason to be afraid. This was probably the only occasion on which I was a little unsure or afraid of them – and then only because I didn't understand.

Again, when I was about twelve, I used to go shopping for my mum in the evening after school. I often got into trouble for taking a long time over it. Unknown to my mum I used to visit the old people's dwellings at the bottom of our road. I'd help the senior citizens, then sit and talk with them, often gaining very interesting information that I'd repeat to my family. They found this very amusing and were sometimes amazed at how I could possibly know all this – especially since it concerned people who were dead. I remember one old lady in particular who told me about herself and how she'd died after suffering from dropsy. I thought she said 'dropped knee' and asked what it was. To my puzzlement she chuckled away to herself and replied, 'Dropped knee is when your knees drop down towards your ankles so that if you sit at the kerbside, you need to sit right back, allowing your feet to hang over the edge of the kerbstone.'

She showed me a picture of herself doing exactly that – sitting down at the kerbside, dangling her feet over the edge into the road and pulling her skirt up over her ankles onto her legs as she did so. To my eyes, her knees had dropped to her ankles. I spent quite a time trying to imagine what that would be like – but because it was time for me to go home, the lady never had a chance to tell me she was joking. So of course I went home and told Mum all about the lady who suffered from dropped knee. She laughed, saying 'Oh Jean, your Dad's right – you have got an over-active imagination. You are funny!' My family, as usual, put the whole thing down to 'another one of Jean's funny stories' designed to make them laugh – which of course they did. No matter how hard I tried I couldn't get them to understand that I really had met this lady; that she was real and not just a figment of my imagination.

This incident comes to mind whenever my pupils or people in general ask me why spirits don't make themselves clearer. Can you imagine the frustration that the old lady must have felt when, try as she might, she couldn't get me to understand what she was talking about. This is one of the reasons why it's vitally important

18

to train our forgotten senses by practising the exercises in this book. Mediums are people – they're fallible. So they make mistakes in transferring information from the spirit world to people's loved ones in this world. The English language is open to misinterpretation as it is, without the added complication of trying to communicate using half-forgotten senses. I'm sure you'll have heard the saying: 'No sense, no feeling'. For example, when a friend is hit on the head by a ball and doesn't react, we'd laughingly say, 'Look. No sense, no feeling!' yet the truth is that we don't actually feel things through these senses. This is easy to understand if we imagine our right hand to be completely without feeling and paralysed. Thus numbed, if we were blindfolded and then someone stuck a pin into our hand we wouldn't feel the pinprick at all. However, if the blindfold was taken off and we were pricked again we wouldn't be one hundred per cent sure that we hadn't felt anything. Or at least we'd flinch when the pin's point came close to our hand. This is because our senses come back into play.

Next time someone close to you is asleep, move your hand slowly towards the bottom of their foot as though you were about to tickle them. You'll be surprised how many times they'll move their foot as you near it. This isn't because they're really awake as it might seem, but because when we are sleeping we have naturally altered our state of consciousness, thereby changing our vibration to a faster one. This is the same vibration – or wavelength, if you like – that we need to communicate with the afterlife because spirits live in the same space as us, but are usually undetectable since they exist on this faster vibration. This is why some who wouldn't claim to be mediums can still obtain information from the spirit world – it comes to them whilst they're sleeping.

Another phenomenon which people find hard to understand is the fact that we can hear silence. Understandable, really, since silence means without sound. But we can hear silence if we try. I'm again talking about using your senses. Imagine turning up at some friends' house just as they were in the middle of an argument with their partner. Even if they pretended things were fine between them, most of us would be aware that something was wrong – even if we couldn't say why. This is because we can sense an awkwardness about them as they pass the silence between them. Sound is the oscillation of the air at particular frequencies which our ears interpret as sound without us consciously realising it.

If a room usually has noises in it and suddenly they're missing we'd notice the difference straight away – even if we couldn't put our finger on exactly what had changed. It's the same with the arguing couple – but how can that be if we can't hear silence? I did say, after all, that they were trying very hard to pretend everything was normal. It's because silence is a sound we can sense – so it is possible to hear it.

I never did manage to erase the lady with 'dropped knees' from my mind and couldn't understand why people didn't believe me. It was only as an adult, realising that I could communicate with spirits, that I actually asked them. That's when I finally found out that the lady was already a spirit back then and that she'd suffered from a condition called 'Dropsy' and had been joking about her knees all along! This changed everything. I asked Mum whether she remembered the incident and was assured that she did. She had a good laugh when I told her the truth behind the story – and it made perfect sense to my family because I've always been naïve!

CHAPTER 3.

Work begins

Maybe it's time for you to start stretching your senses. If we ask most people how many senses they have they'll probably say five, which of course are:

* Sight

* Hearing

* Smell

* Taste

* Touch

They're forgetting the most important of all – and that's aware-ness of our aura. This is most important because with it we can be aware of many things around us – by which I mean both here and in the spirit world. For those of you who don't know what an aura is, I'll explain briefly.

We all have a magnetic energy field around our bodies – this is what we mean by an aura. If you were sitting alone in a room and someone came up silently from behind, the chances are you'd notice them coming before they actually touched you. This is because you'd have sensed them. Your aura enables you to do this. As soon as someone touches this magnetic field, a minor shock takes place – like a little electrical surge. Sometimes we're not sure what has affected our aura – but simply know that something has – but actually you can train yourself to be aware of why and how this happens.

Many years ago people had no televisions, radios or computers to occupy their time – phones with which to call up anyone, anywhere, any time they like. People had no choice but to make use of what was available to them – so they made much more use of their senses. As I mentioned earlier, I rarely watched television as a child. We didn't have a phone either. I was brought up being told not to speak unless I was spoken to and, since my siblings and I would always do what our father told us, we learned very quickly how to say a lot with just a look. One glance could speak volumes!

In fact we were using our senses. Sight, being a sense we're all used to, can help if you take the time to look properly. But if you add to that a feeling we can all pick up on, like anger, it's a different story. If you were unfortunate enough to be deaf just the sight of someone talking quickly and going red in the face would tell you that they were telling someone off. You'd be sure of this even though you hadn't heard a thing. If that person were looking directly at you, you'd know you were on the receiving end of a scolding. It's all common sense – yet people don't seem to realise that they can take it a step further. If you were to ask yourself, 'how does this make me feel?', you'd immediately know the answer. You'd feel angry, upset, belittled or all manner of other reactions, depending whether you knew why you were being told-off and whether or not you felt you deserved it. You're probably wondering what all this has to do with the spirit world or even auras, come to that. Well, I'm coming to that.

I'd like you to adapt part of your everyday life. I'm not suggesting that you stop watching television or using the telephone or anything similarly hard to keep up. But I am going to ask you to follow a few simple steps for a few weeks. By then I feel that I'll have piqued your natural interest and that you'll want to carry on learning how to use your other senses.

I suggest that this moment is a new beginning for you. It's the start of real communication with yourself and others around you. Step one is to humour me by having an open mind and accepting a new beginning – and being aware of that new beginning. I'm asking you to try, for once, not to be oblivious to your own needs and your surroundings as most of us are.

Tomorrow morning, when you first wake up, I want you to take the time to ask:

'What is today going to be like?'

Many of you will raise the first stumbling block here by saying they don't have the time. Not true. I'm one of the busiest people I know and suffer a great deal of pain along the way which slows me down in some activities and prevents me taking part in others. Yet I find the time for myself and for the spirit world because it's important. It does help to make the suffering easier to cope with – and to help other people along the way. You don't have to put any time aside – you could actually ask yourself this question whilst you're rushing around, getting ready for the day ahead. I don't expect you to know straight away what's about to happen because sometimes it's a very subtle feeling – if you're not careful you could miss it.

If, for instance, you had a sudden sense of rushing around and you were doing just that at the time, it would be easy to mistake this new feeling for something more mundane – when it's actually the answer to that question!

That's the main reason for asking you to do this exercise. When people first begin to develop senses that have become dormant through lack of use they're often sure that nothing is happening.

In fact, a good friend of mine called Laureece, says that she is oblivious to the spirit world, but the truth is that she has exceptional ability and understanding in this area. The trouble is that half the time she simply doesn't listen to what her senses are telling her.

The title of this book came to me when she told me she was oblivious to the spirit world and Izeakial said:

'That's a good title for your book: "Oblivious but True"'

I'm asking you to learn to trust yourself. I promise, it's the most difficult thing I'll ask of you.

Now, as you go about your life's business, I want you to pay more attention to the people with whom you come into contact. I'm asking you to listen to what people are not saying. This may sound back-to-front but it does make a lot of sense once you understand it. For example, if you know someone very well, you begin to realise that they don't always mean exactly what they say – often because they don't want to bore you with their problems.

If someone asks me, 'How are you?', I quite often respond with, 'I am fine thank you.'

My answer is my way of hiding the fact that things aren't so good. On the other hand, if my reply is:

'All right thank you' or 'Great, thank you.'

Then things are going great in my part of the world. Good friends of mine such as Laureece now interpret the phrase, 'I am fine thanks' to mean precisely the opposite. They are, you see, listening to what I am not saying!

People who know me well know that I am very good at listening to what other people are not saying although I very rarely let people know my innermost thoughts and feelings on any given subject. In other words, just because I don't reveal that I know something, doesn't mean I don't know it. This probably sounds strange yet familiar to most people – because we all hide our feelings to a certain extent. When we are communicating with the spirit world this comes in very handy. If, for instance, I wanted to pass on a very personal message to someone from the their loved ones in the spirit world and we were with others at the time, I would need to express the information in a way that was comprehensible only to the person for whom it was intended. This becomes easier once you're used to it.

Because all these signs and senses are hard to get used to, people tend to give up trying. I'm asking you to have patience. If any of this is not making sense to you at the moment, I assure you that it does get easier. If listening to what people are not saying sounds a bit deep and unusual to you it's understandable because you haven't been guided in life by the spirit world like I have.

It was only a few years ago that I became aware that not everyone sees the spirit people. Since that realisation I've bombarded them with questions – and I'm pleased to say they've answered them! I did learn at about twelve or thirteen that thoughts were living things and that if you asked sincerely for something to happen it would.

One day, Chris and I were playing at jumping across the brook on our way home from the shops. As I went to jump, I missed my footing and landed with my foot in the water. As I took off my shoe and sock, Chris laughed and said she'd tell Mum – because we weren't allowed to go near the brook. I asked Izeakial to make something happen to stop her telling Mum. Immediately, Chris tried to kick a stone into the brook and her shoe flew off and splashed into the water! Needless to say, she didn't tell Mum after that (we have told her now, after reaching adulthood!). Another time, one evening after school, Chris and I were on our way to the shops when we noticed a commotion over by the same brook at the bottom of our road. Crossing over, we found that a girl and a boy from our school were stuck in the mud - a kind of sinking sand had formed from sand dumped by builders from a nearby site. The fire brigade was called and soon the girl was freed. The boy, however, was still sinking in the mire and I could see that the firemen were getting very worried – so I asked Izeakial for help. Suddenly, the firemen were able to pull the boy from the mud, leaving behind a single forlorn Wellington boot. I know that the sceptics will say this is mere coincidence – but the fact is that things like this have been happening around me all my life.

November 9th of the year I turned fifteen is one date I'll never forget. My parents had been out for the evening and, at about ten-thirty, while I was making the most of the rare free time and watching 'The Invaders' on television my father suddenly burst in. Mum was about to give birth to the baby she was expecting. I was to run to my friend's house next door but one and ask them to call an ambulance. Arriving breathless at their door, I found that my friend and her parents were out. Her nineteen year old brother was in, however and, overcoming my initial embarrass-ment at having to broach what I felt was a delicate subject with a boy, I asked him to make the call and scurried home. |To my delight my brother Martin was born the following day. But death too reared its ugly head: on that same day we found our budgie, which had been part of the family for a long time, lying dead. Then, to make matters worse we went outside to feed our rabbit – only to find him dead too. That may sound fairly trivial to an adult – but it's no laughing matter to a fifteen-year-old who's afraid of dying. Now I was preoccupied with birth and death all at once; dealing with feeling happy and sad at the same time. That's something I still find hard to this day.

The following year my friend from next door but one sudden-ly lost her father to the spirit world. He simply went out to work, had a heart attack and never came back. My friend was especial-ly close to her father – and I was close to him too, having spent a lot of time at their house. The experience changed her – she grew up almost overnight and I was left once again to cope with the aftermath of bereavement and the changes it brings. Life never follows the same pattern once a death has occurred; the changes can be minor or dramatic, but they're changes all the same. Somehow life goes on – although in a different way. Later that year another neighbour died suddenly after collapsing in a bus shelter – a girl we'd all played with as we grew up. She was only eighteen.

It was as if my whole life was taken over by people dying – making me feel very confused and afraid of death almost to the point of feeling guilty for still being alive myself. Over the years, while all these things were going on, I had come to rely more and more on my conversations with three particular people in my life: Izeakial, the most important of all, Amy and of course the nurse.

On first meeting Izeakial one of the things I noticed was his close-shaven beard, stern look and staring eyes which could be misinterpreted as hard. He may be hard – but he's fair. He answers every question I ask – as long as he feels I can't come up with the answer on my own. For example, if I've mislaid something, he'll tell me where it is only if I've made every effort to find it and have failed. This brings me to a question I'm often asked by people who are developing their spiritual side:

'I don't know whether it's them or me. How can I tell the difference?'

This is not an easy one to answer in simple terms – so I asked my guide to answer it. His reply was:

'My child, there is a simple answer to all your questions. If you were capable of taking a look at your brain it would read just like a map. Do you understand?'

I smiled as the thought crossed my mind and replied, 'Yes, I do.' Izeakial immediately started talking again:

'Good. I am sure that you will have noticed that I always stand behind your right shoulder whenever you are talking to me through your senses.'

'Yes I have', I said, with a rush of excitement that spurred me to answer aloud, which is unusual for me, knowing full well that spirits communicate telepathically and don't need you to voice your thoughts.

'I stand on your right,' he continued, 'because we communicate with people who have not yet passed over through their brains. Everyone's brain has a left and right portion – each of which control the opposite sides of the body. Now then, on the left hand side of your brain there is a part we call the subliminal. This is towards the front, above and slightly forward of the ear. Because we use this part to communicate with people who are unsure that we are here, we stand behind them because the subliminal part is at the front, and to the right, because the relevant part is to the left. You see opposites attract in this situation, making it easier for us to communicate.'

I knew that he had stopped to see my reaction. I also knew that there was no need to answer.

'Subliminal messages were used in advertising for many years in times gone by. For instance, a word saying the name of a product that a company wanted to advertise would appear in front of the newsreader's face on television. This word would be made up of tiny dots which, though invisible to the human eye, would be picked up by the subliminal part of our brain. Then, when we saw this product for sale, we would be tempted to try it without knowing why. This is no longer allowed in advertising because it is considered to be a form of brainwashing. In fact it is illegal.'

At this point he gave me one of the half-smiles I'd become familiar with and went on,

'However, this is one of the main ways for us in the spirit world to communicate with you when we cannot make you aware of us in any other way. This is why people sometimes get an idea in their heads for no apparent reason. The information is supplied in such a way that we are sure that it will be heard – not that we mean to tell you what to do, just to guide you. Everyone has a personal responsibility for themselves In other words, they're in charge of their own life – not us. We cannot take this responsibility away from you and you should not want us to.'

He was making sense of things which had previously been hard to understand but I still didn't feel that he'd answered my question. Before I had a chance to say so, he continued,

'The answer to your question, my child, is within each individual. When you feel you have received information from the spirit world you must immediately put your senses backwards by placing this thought in your mind: 'Who is it behind me saying that?' By doing so you automatically put the information where it came from – behind you. Straight away you will become aware of something else – maybe purely a sense of someone or something being there. Now place a new thought in your brain:

'Are you male or female?'

These may sound simple but once you have trained your brain to respond in this way then – and only then – are you beginning to take notice of a sense to which we in the spirit world have easy access. I promise you that the information which I have just passed on to you from the spirit world does make a lot of sense.'

At first I had to practise what he had told me – because I'd grown used to communicating with these people so naturally, I didn't realise how it was done – like many of you. Although to begin with the opportunities to practise this method will be few and far between, please stick with it because, I promise you, it does get easier with practice. You will also find that the more you use this way of linking with the spirit world, the more they will talk to you. After all, if you were to talk to someone and received no reply, would you keep up a one-sided conversation for very long? I suspect not.

I have now asked you to do two things which, although simple, can be frustrating to start off with. Practise them at every chance you get. Just to remind you, they are:

1. When you wake up in the morning, ask yourself, 'What is today going to be like?'

If you have time to write down any thoughts or feelings you experience in response to this you'll be surprised how much it can help. You will suddenly become aware that you actually know quite a lot – and this realisation boosts your confidence that you can do this.

2. Every time a thought comes into your head for no apparent reason send your thoughts and feelings backwards. Do this by simply placing questions into your head about who is communicating with you, instead of just thinking, 'Why did I think that?' or 'Was that me?'

Remember that trust is the hardest part of getting to know the spirit world. You will find that trust in the knowledge that the spirit world exists will come to you more easily than trust in yourself – or in the fact that you can do it at all. One more piece of advice which you'll find helpful is <u>do not think whilst you link.</u> This isn't easy – you'll be surprised how much of a habit it has become to think. And habits are hard to break. Instead of pondering what you've observed and why, try focusing on whom it is and how they have managed to get close enough to communicate with you.

One of the most important steps with your development at this point is to stretch your senses. This means paying attention to the five familiar senses we all know about – which may seem strange considering that it's spiritual development you're aiming for. I assure you, though, that they will help in the long run.

You need two people for these exercises – and I'll talk you through them as if two people were following them. It's important to follow these steps in the given order, resisting the temptation to skip one here and there. I can assure you that this is for your benefit – not mine, the spirit world's or anyone else's come to that.

For the first exercise you will need:

* An ordinary scarf or similar (for use as a blindfold)

* A set of headphones through which you can play music

* A wall with space for one person to stand up against it

* At least two people

Now we can begin:

1. Both remove your shoes

2. Decide which of you will wear the headphones and blindfold first (you both get a turn)

3. One of you now puts on the blindfold and headphones with music playing – so that you can't see or hear anything happening around you. It doesn't matter what kind of music as long as you can hear it and it's loud enough to drown out other sounds in the room.

4. With the help and guidance of the person who can see, the blindfolded person stands facing the wall and places the open palms of their hands against it.

5. After giving the blindfolded person a moment or two to relax them, the person who can see quietly steps behind their partner, moving as close as possible without actually touching them.

6. Then they slowly and quietly touch the blindfolded person on the shoulder. This should be repeated several times, altering the timing and or the shoulder they touch so that the blindfolded person cannot tell when and where the next

touch will be.

7. During this process, the blindfolded person should say when they feel the touch or when they are aware that they are <u>about to be touched.</u>

8. Both partners should have several goes at being the one to test their senses.

9. When the experiment is finished, both of you should make a note of the results, recording the date and time (this will be important later when you need to check on your progress).

This exercise is good for heightening the use of our senses. These ought to be fully alert in order to protect us from any approaching danger from behind but since we rarely make use of this ability, it tends to weaken. Reawakening this faculty not only strengthens these senses but also makes it easier for us to sense spirits when they are close to us – thereby taking us a step closer to spirit linking.

In these early days of training our senses the headphones and blindfold should be our almost constant companions – whether separately or together. Most people would benefit from some time wearing a blindfold – it would sharpen their senses.

According to my guides in the spirit world every medium is 'clairsentient'. Some are 'clairsentient' alone while others are 'clairaudient' or clairvoyant' as well. Some, like me, are lucky enough to be all three. These words actually mean clear sensing, clear hearing and clear seeing in that order – they're all expressions familiar to those following a spiritual path. Clairsentience, or clear sensing, is by far the hardest form of spirit communication to learn and to understand. It's also the most important. This is because it's the easiest for the spirits to use, providing them with many ways of transmitting information to our senses. If someone from the spirit realm stood close behind us we would sense a presence even if we didn't know what it was – or why it was there. People who aren't sufficiently spiritually developed to read the signs tend to describe this sensation in various ways. They may report a sudden quivering sensation radiating all over their body and often describe it as a 'spooky' feeling. This is unfortunate because the word 'spooky' conjures up all sorts of false ideas about the spirit world and its inhabitants' intentions. An experienced medium, on receiving this shivery sensation, would immediately be aware that someone from the spirit world had stood next to them. That person, I can assure you, is only announcing their presence and expressing their love. A student, on the other hand may not be sure what to think. They might say that more likely than not, the spirits are with them. But that's all they could be sure of because they wouldn't be used to their own bodies or using their senses – which are, after all, among their bodies' most important functions.

At this point it's time for you to involve a third person in the exercise if possible. Repeat the exercise as before but with two people approaching the blindfolded person from behind. Moving simultaneously they should approach on either side, each touching the shoulder nearest them. Once the blindfolded person has got used to this happening, go back to just one person touching them on both shoulders and see if it's noticed. The blindfolded person must call out straight away when they are aware of anything – no matter how subtle the awareness. They should also state which side they feel the touch. With practice you'll all be at least a little bit aware when someone is approaching you from behind – and then it's time to change the exercise completely. That may seem a strange thing to do but I assure you that it will help to heighten your senses and take you a step closer to knowing when spirits are with you.

As far as clairaudience is concerned, many people don't realise how difficult it is for spirits to produce the sound – and very few know how they do it. Quite often, when people are meditating or linking with spirits they suddenly begin to cough uncontrollably.

It's not because they've got a cold coming – it's because spirits make sound by vibrating our own voice boxes. While they're doing this they tend to come in very close to us, creating a tickling sensation that makes us cough. There's a simple remedy – just ask them to stand back a bit! It's because spirits use our voice box to 'speak' that mediums say that they feel that they haven't heard the sound with their ears – but as a voice, usually emanating from a place slightly forward from their throat and a little to the right.

CHAPTER 4

A changing world

Leaving school was something of a mixed blessing for me. A year earlier, on the evening of Chris' last day at school (she's thirteen months older than me), we were sitting on the back garden see-saw that dad made us, just chatting about life in general. As darkness began to fall she told me how excited she was at the prospect of getting a job and having some money of her own to spend. Of course I was pleased for her but wished that my turn would hurry up and come along. After all, we'd done most things together all our lives.

Although we're still close, Chris was of course living a different life now. She was going out with Derek, her first boyfriend, to whom she's now married. A year later it was my turn to leave school – but by now my feelings had changed. I wasn't too sure about getting a job or about leaving either. Actually my father had asked me not to get a job for a while because my mum needed help with my baby brother, the housework, cooking and shopping. At first I didn't mind this too much because my baby brother Martin was a gorgeous little child and I loved him from the start – despite the fact that the rabbit and budgie's deaths had coincided with his birth.

I quite enjoyed taking my sister Hazel to school, bringing her home and picking up the shopping on the bike my father had bought me for my fourteenth birthday. I was very proud of my brand new light blue bicycle – probably because it had been bought for me and wasn't the usual hand-me-down.

There was, however, a story attached to the bike. When I was about thirteen and a half, a really nice lady who lived a few doors away asked me if I wanted an old bike, which was on top of her shed. Of course I jumped at the chance and went round to fetch the cycle, whose brakes, she'd warned, needed looking at. Chris and I had a look at the brakes but, I must admit, that even after our attention they still didn't work properly. Anyway, as far as we were concerned that was what feet were for! However, one night while I was playing on my bike outside our house my father arrived home early. And he was not pleased. But he could see how upset I was when he banned me from riding it, so he promised that if I didn't ride it he'd buy me a new one for my fourteenth birthday. I stopped riding the bike, Dad put it on top of our shed and, true to his word, bought me a new one on my birthday.

My first day's riding was marred, however, by the fact that Chris didn't have a bike of her own. After a brief discussion, we decided that if she rode the old one, Dad might buy her a new one too. The plan didn't work – although we had a lot of fun before Dad took it away from her. One day we decided to cycle to Sutton Town Centre, about two miles away. To get there we had to go down the very steep Redicap Hill, which was fine until we reached the bottom and the fact that Chris had no brakes gained new importance. The theory was that I'd ride in front so that I could help her to slow down – not one of my better plans! I braked and slowed down, putting out my right arm to stop Chris as she went past. Chris rammed her feet down onto the road in a vain attempt to brake – but unfortunately she was going too fast and went careering past at great speed, sparks flying from her feet as she went. Suddenly I saw the nurse guide appear, stepping out to catch Chris's bike. Looking back, we're convinced that Chris only avoided being killed or badly injured by a miracle – spirits to the rescue once again!

I should point out though, that had it been Chris's time to go to the spirit side of life, the spirits would not have been allowed to help. This had been proved to me by something that happened to my brother Ken. On Whit Sunday the year before my brother's death, my Mum, Dad, brothers and sisters, my dad's friend and I went to the Lichfield Bower. For those who've never heard of this, it's an annual funfair held in the streets of Lichfield. At the time, my Father owned a car but it wasn't big enough for all of us so some of us caught a bus, then a train and met the rest of them at the fair.

Heading home after a wonderful day, we caught the train to Sutton and headed for the bus stop by the side of the Empress cinema which, sadly, is no more. By the bus stop was a four foot wall, on the other side of which was a stairwell leading to a door – making the drop on the other side a good twenty feet. Ken and Keith were sitting on the wall, while I leaned against it. During a bout of horseplay atop the wall, Ken toppled backwards, falling head first over the other side. Luckily I saw this out of the corner of my eye and with a reflex action caught him by the ankle as he dropped which broke his fall. Had his fall been unbroken he'd definitely have died. This was June 1970. Just eight months later on February 26th, 1971 Kenneth died. So you see, the time has be right for us to pass over to the spirit world – and when that fall happened a few months before Ken's death, the time wasn't right.

The nurse in the spirit world about whom I've talked has been there with me for many more situations like this and she's played an important part in my life and those of my children. When changes, sometimes drastic ones, happen in life, she has always tried to help me to understand their meaning. To help you get used to differences, both here and in the spirit world, simple exercises are occasionally necessary. This next exercise can help you to notice subtle changes on your senses. As well as the blindfold, you'll need several household objects, such as a key, scissors etc. To keep things simple, I'll refer to the group members as 'A', 'B' and 'C'.

1. Person A should put on the blindfold (you can be seated for this exercise)

2. Either B or C now passes an object to A, who examines it by touch.

3. Person A then describes what they think the object is and what it's made of. B or C then write down this response, noting the accuracy or otherwise of A's description.

4. Each person takes a turn at being blindfolded and describing various objects. The objects must be presented in a different order each time – or ideally, should be different objects altogether – so that memory can't interfere.

As I've said before and will probably say again, thinking is your worst enemy while you're trying to link with the spirit world. So I repeat: do not think while you link. It's a good code of practice to adhere to. That may sound odd but let me give you an example. Imagine I ask you to memorise the room you're in because, in a moment, I am going to blindfold you and ask you to walk across the room unaided and sit down in the chair opposite. When I blindfold you, the chances are that you will do very well in the experiment. Imagine then that I repeat the exercise several times using different subjects and allowing the rest of the group to watch. Each subject would appear more confident than the last, but if when it came to their turn, I placed a chair in front of them after the blindfold was on, they'd walk straight into it. It wouldn't cross their mind that something might be blocking their way. This is purely because thought came into the situation whilst this repetition was taking place – changing the situation from what it was to what they thought it might be. This alone made them fail the exercise. I hope that this helps to define the points that I am trying to make. These people would definitely have used a little more caution whilst crossing that room, thereby paying more attention to the realities, if thought had not come into the equation.

While I was training to be a medium I tended to pay full attention to everything because I realised how much I'd missed as a child, having failed to appreciate even the possibility of the spirit world's existence. At this point I must interject my own line of thought, just to say that friends are invaluable assets to your development – you need them to practice with and on! Without my friends I would not have persevered and I owe them a lot. One day a practice sitting with a friend was going extremely well until I asked her whether her mother had fallen down the stairs at some point before she died. She replied immediately, 'No she didn't.' This surprised me. Why, then, was that scene so clear to me? She looked equally puzzled so I asked her, 'Well if that's the case, why am I seeing a clear picture of your mother sitting at the foot of the stairs among a pile of shoes?'

A big smile came onto her face as she answered, 'Now I understand!' I was pleased that at least she understood, but nevertheless puzzled. She went on, 'When my mother was a small child she would spend hours sitting at the foot of the stairs playing with the shoes that were kept there. When she grew elderly and senile, her thoughts reverted to childhood and once again she would sit at the bottom of the stairs playing with shoes!' This incident taught me a valuable lesson: do not think whilst you link.

I'm sure you can see how easy it would be to make that kind of mistake. All I did was to change the information I was given by adding my own interpretation. This changed the whole message, making the information appear wrong when in fact it was correct. I was wrong. The moral of this story is: never try to work out why the spirit world is showing what it's showing you. Just tell it exactly as it is. If you do this, you'll be surprised how accurate your messages will become with practice. This is important for the person receiving the sitting – but even more important for the loved one who's communicating from the spirit world. They are coming through with a desperate need to let their loved ones know that they are here to visit, bringing support, love guidance and whatever else is needed. Sometimes people who visit a medium, be it on a rostrum during a public meeting or in private, do so because they have a great need to believe that we do not die but live on in the spirit world. Their life at that moment may be going through a bad patch or perhaps they have lost someone important to them to the spirit world. Yet their upbringing leads them to be sceptical about our beliefs – perhaps to the extent of seeing us as evil. The way to begin to change those beliefs is to convince them that maybe their loved one really is here. Notice that I use the words 'maybe' and 'might'. This is because that is how you start. As their confidence in you and what you are telling them grows, they will begin to realise that there's nothing evil about it. We do, after all, work with love.

It is important to point out that the spirit world lives in the same space as we do – just on a much faster vibration, which the human eye can't see. To speed up our vibration, we need to concentrate great love on the unseen or unknown as people call it. I hope that when you have read this book and practised a few exercises you too will know that the spirit world really does exist and they really do visit us.

Mediums are often asked why it is that most of the great mediums of our time have suffered, both physically and mentally. The usual answer is that mediums need to have sympathy and empathy for the people with whom they come into contact. Pain comes their way so that they will understand how it feels to suffer when dealing with people with similar problems. Although this answers the question, it doesn't make much sense to me. I wouldn't trust a spirit world that made me suffer just to make me understand. So I asked Izeakial for the real reason. His answer sat more easily with me:

'A lot of people are born with the ability to be mediums but the time has to be right for them to actually use the gift. The way to link with the spirit world is by sending great love from within, which in turn relaxes you deep inside and raises your vibration.

When a person is unhappy, they naturally send their thoughts deep within themselves which in turn relaxes them deep inside. They do this in the hope that everyone and everything else is shut out – which of course is the very action necessary to change our vibration. Because this person has dealt with a lot of sad, scary or lonely moments they naturally learn how to change their vibration at will. I would like, however, to explain that when exceptionally good things happen to us, they have the same effect. For instance, those who are lucky enough to see a new baby just after birth – that is, within a day or two – will know what I mean when I say that as you look at the baby everything and everyone else in the room seems to disappear for a few seconds as you gaze at this little miracle. This is because you have naturally changed your vibration.

Unhappy times are more obvious because people tend to remember them more than they remember the tiny miracles. It's not because the miracles are less important – it's purely because heartache leaves a lasting impression which is easily recalled at other sad times.'

This answer satisfied me because I know for a fact that I'd often be aware of these spirit visitors whilst I was unhappy, worried or feeling alone in a very large world. You see, a medium works well with spirits because he or she has suffered – not because the spirit world has made him or her suffer.

If you are following the direction in which we're heading, I hope you'll be aware that I'm trying to teach the retraining of your natural ability to sense without physically using your ears. Next, I would like to introduce you to an exercise, which uses the sense of smell. For this you'll need the blindfold, as before, and some aromatic substances such as soap, perfume, coffee or curry powder. Now follow these steps:

1 Put the blindfold on person A

2. B or C should now hold one of the strong-smelling substances directly under A's nose. A then describes what substance it is, while the others write down those responses. Even wrong answers are important and need to be remembered.

3. Repeat the process with several different substances

4. Now take something with a strong smell and hold it close behind A's head without touching. This is to test whether they are aware of a smell coming from behind them. This may sound silly but it is important because spirits quite often stand close behind us to be within our auric field. They also regularly put a waft of aroma into the air to tell us something.

5. If A is not already sitting on a chair with room to walk around it, they should be gently moved to such a position. This is because you need to be able to approach them from all directions. Remember that spirits can do this wherever we are. Walls etc. are not a problem for them.

6. Now it's time for B or C to hold the next item further away, repeating this with several of the aromas.

7. As B steps up with the next odour, a cup of coffee for instance, C should whisper loud enough for A to hear, 'That tea smells good.' You'll be surprised how difficult it is for you to adjust immediately. This adjustment is, of course,

necessary as you decide whether it is your nose or your ears offering the correct answer. I promise you that while spirit linking you will need to do this sort of thing all the time. It does get easier with practice.

8. These exercises must be repeated using different odours and or in a different order for B and C, remembering, of course, to write everything down.

You will be surprised how often this causes confusion. You'll also be surprised how certain you are that you're right when you're actually wrong. If you do falter before answering the question, it's still worth noting because your hesitation shows doubt, which shows that you were thinking. If someone from the spirit world is impressing something on your brain it is very straightforward until you start to think about what you already know. Then you change the message and get it wrong. This is why some mediums say that they can't give someone in their own family a message. The truth is that they can – it just becomes a lot harder because their own knowledge interrupts the message. So you see, these exercises are vital training in linking properly.

The mistakes that arise are not the fault of the person in the spirit world but ours because we falter before expressing what we have received. Some of you may be feeling a bit daunted by all this, to say the least – but please don't let it put you off. The more practice you have, the more confident you will get and the easier it all becomes. Practice, after all, makes perfect in spirit linking just like everything else! I can also assure you that spirits will help you when they can. So please learn to trust them and yourself. As I've said before, trust in them and in yourself are the two hardest things to learn.

As I mentioned Aromas before, I should explain that one of the easiest things for the Spirit world to do, is to release an Aroma that they hope we will recognise, into the air. For instance, if it is likely that you would remember that your Grandfather smoked, then it is natural that if you smell cigarette smoke in a room where nobody is smoking, then you will think of him. This is also a very easy way for them to communicate with a person who is not generally aware of Spirit.

I am sure many of the people who are reading this book will have at some time, been out for the day and stopped to buy fish and chips to eat in the car? You eat the food and throw the paper away in the bin, before setting off to finish the journey. But I guarantee that the next time you get into the car after it has been locked up for a while, it will smell of fish and chips? This is because the molecules that make up the car, such as the steering wheel, seats, roof, etc., cling on to the aroma releasing it again as soon as there is any movement like us getting into the car. The smell is then picked up by your nasal passages.

Every person has an Aura around them, as I have said before, which is a magnetic field. If someone from the Spirit World releases an Aroma towards somebody's Aura and then that person moves, the smell is released and picked up by the person's nasal passages, just like the fish and chips in the molecules that make up the car.

The only problem is that after a bit of thought many people decide that it is their imagination. Which is a terrible shame when their loved one has tried so hard to communicate.

CHAPTER 5

Starting out

It's now time to return to the sense-stretching exercises. Sadly, most people who develop themselves spiritually don't like clairsentience because they think it's the hardest element to learn and understand. If only they'd give it enough time I'm sure they'd find it as easy as the rest. Yes, I did say easy. We're the ones who make things difficult! If we try too hard, it becomes hard – because we're not listening to our senses, which appear to be silent. Once again, therefore, I'm asking you to listen to what people are not saying – this time the people concerned are in the spirit world rather than here.

As I've already said, all mediums are clairsentient. Tackling the use of your sense, therefore, is vital if you are to move forward. This form of communication can be used in many ways but first of all we need to get used to the idea that we can feel sound as well as hear it. We can also see it. I'm sure that most of you will have noticed some people who can't hear what another is saying without seeing their face. On the face of it, they're lip reading. But this has nothing to do with it. The real reason is that when facing the direction from which the sound is coming, they can sense the sound vibration. I've never forgotten one afternoon while I was taking a church service, when I found that I couldn't see or hear the spirit world but could only sense it. I was horrified because I'd always found this way of linking very difficult. That night I told off one of my guides about this – only to be told in turn by Izeakial:

'My child, you are not using all of the gifts that you have been given in order to communicate with us properly. If you learn how to talk to us through Clairsentience we will return the other two methods. This, I promise you, my child.'

I was amazed by this but went out of my way to learn and practice communication by clairsentience very quickly. I now find this method as easy as seeing or hearing the spirit world, although I must admit that it makes you work harder.

At this point I would like to suggest again that you try to communicate with your guides for a few minutes every night as you are about to go to bed and again each morning when you wake up. It doesn't matter whether or not you are aware of them because they will be aware of you. Equally it's not a problem if you fall asleep whilst you're doing this or if you're rushing around getting ready for your day. You don't need to talk aloud or stop what you are doing. They will hear you and eventually make you aware that they are communicating back.

You will be impressed by the results of this next exercise once you check them. You need at least two people - A and B – standing about three feet apart.

A should stand facing B but B should stand sideways on. In other words, A should be looking at the side of B's face and body.

1. A should mumble under his or her breath a sentence of their own choice. This should not be a whisper but it shouldn't be too loud either.

2. Now B should try to repeat that sentence.

3. Person B now turns to face person A

4. A now repeats the sentence they said before – or a different sentence if the first one was heard.

5. Now A and B change places.

6. Remember to write down the results.

It is amazing how many people cannot hear a low voice whilst facing away from its source. Yet the same person hears perfectly well when facing the sound's source. For me, most of the exercises came naturally – they were all part of growing up. As I've said before, I quite liked spending time with my younger sisters and brothers. There was baby Martin and four year old Gordon at home and Hazel – who was only five but went to school. Keith and Kenneth, then aged ten and eight were also at school at that time. Hazel had a little boyfriend who lived in one of the police houses at the top of our road because his dad was a policeman. His mum and I used to chat while taking the children to school, after which I would cross the road to do the shopping and then go home on my bike. Although the greater part of the day was taken up with housework and looking after children, I really didn't mind. In fact I even enjoyed it. What I didn't enjoy was my dad and sisters' return from work because I was then expected to wait on them hand and foot. This meant that I rarely had time to myself and never got to watch a television programme from beginning to end. Sometimes I'd give up on TV and take my bike outside – not to ride it, but to sit on it at our gate talking to Amy.

One evening I was about to watch Coronation Street when Pam asked me to make her a cup of tea – to which I replied that I was watching television and that she should make her own. She replied that since I was the only one who didn't work it was my job to make the tea, which annoyed me intensely because I'd been on the go all day – like every other day, in fact. That evening I told my father that I wanted to get a job. He was quite surprised and asked me why. I explained what had happened and said that although I could see my sister's point of view, I worked hard all day without pay. Dad told Pam that if he gave me permission to get a job I'd get one straight away. Indignantly she retorted that I wouldn't. Dad's response was to say, 'All right then Bean (this was his nickname for me), you can get a job.'

The next day I did just that. I found myself a job and had Pam to thank for moving me forward in life.

We went out together quite a lot after that – sometimes in a foursome with our boyfriends. I believe that this was the spirit world's way of changing my life and bringing Pam and I closer. If so, they certainly succeeded!

Starting work was a refreshing change – even though my lack of qualifications meant factory work was the only kind available to me. Dad gave Pam and I a lift part of the way to work and we'd complete the journey by bus. Although we worked in different places they were quite close to each other, so we always met up to travel together back to where Dad could meet us and give us a lift home. Dad said that this was safer than us having to carry too much money with us to work – so I would carry just enough for the return bus fare and no more. Then, the sudden death by heart attack of an exceptionally nice and spiritual colleague called Henry Smith came as a great shock to me. I was particularly affected by his death because he'd always been kind to me. They had a collection in his memory at work and although I had only enough for my bus fare to donate. This was more substantial than usual because Dad wasn't meeting us that day and I had enough to pay for two bus rides. That night I asked Pam to lend me the bus fare home, pointing out that I had enough money at home to repay her. She didn't lend me it but instead agreed to walk with me.

This incident made me aware that when a death occurs, no matter how slight the impact, if you are connected to the person who has passed; lives all around are affected by their death. Obviously, the closer you are to them, the more your life will be affected.

Another evening, on leaving work, I had to travel home alone because my sister had changed jobs and my father was off work through illness. I made my way to the bus stop on this cold, dark, foggy and rainy night, thinking as I went about Coronation Street on television. This was because a character called Val Barlow had received an electric shock from her iron and that night we were to find out whether she was dead or alive. I was keen to get home in time to see it! Typically, like so many of the best-laid plans, this one went wrong. I saw a bus approaching and squinted against the fog and rain in an attempt to see if it was the one I wanted: the 114. Just as I was thinking, 'Thank goodness for that,' on realising that it was my bus, the people in the queue shoved me forward. Stumbling up into the vehicle I dropped my money into the driver's tray and made my way to the back where there was just one seat free with its back to the window. I sat, people-watching, as the bus drew away, happy to be on my way home at last.

After I'd been on the bus for about twenty minutes it began to empty and I moved to a window seat so that I could look out. Rubbing the condensation from the window and peering out I could see fields and trees but, worryingly, I didn't recognise any of them. I was on the wrong bus! Panicked, I jumped off the bus without thinking at the next stop, only to find that I was in a small and completely unfamiliar village. There was a phone booth. But of course I was penniless. Although fifteen, I was still very naïve – as you'll see from what happened next. I dialled 999! The police were exceptionally kind and understanding and told me to stay put and wait for a policeman to come and help me. When the constable arrived he took me to the police station, which turned out to be a little house just across the road. Apparently I'd caught the 116 by mistake and ended up in Kingsbury. The police decided to take me to the nearest bus station – Tamworth – and told me to give the bus driver my name and address. It was very dark by now and all thoughts of Coronation Street were forgotten. Feeling a little afraid at being alone in a strange place at night, never having travelled far before, I was very pleased when at last the bus pulled into the station. I wasn't so happy when the driver told me that because I had no means of identification he wouldn't let me board without any money.

At that moment a police car passed. I flagged it down and told the policeman about my predicament. He very kindly lent me half a crown (about twelve and a half pence in today's money) and smilingly gave me his name and the address of his police station so that I could return it. I hurriedly boarded the bus, which eventually dropped me near Sutton Town Centre, about two miles from our house. I ran most of the way home and, as I turned from the gullyway, halfway up the street into Lingard Road, where we lived, I saw lots of people. They started cheering.

It turned out that they'd got up a search party to look for me because I was never late in coming home. They were extremely pleased to see me – particularly because of a recent news story about a girl of my age who'd gone missing and been found murdered. My father was angry at first because I hadn't thought to make a reverse charge call to our neighbours. I explained that this hadn't occurred to me and, when he saw how scared I was, he softened, gave me a hug and told me to come home and have my tea. I was so relieved to be home that I didn't mind my family being a bit put out at having had to miss Coronation Street. As usual, when I was afraid, the nurse was at hand – and I said to her, 'I do wish my family could have seen Coronation Street.' She just smiled and comforted me. But to everyone's surprise it was announced the next day that they would be re-showing Monday night's episode of Coronation because reception had been impaired by the poor weather. Just as the announcement finished, the nurse fleetingly appeared, smiled and was gone. Needless to say we all got to see the programme after all!

I sent the money back to the kind policeman as promised and received a lovely letter back, thanking me for my honesty because he hadn't expected to hear from me again. So that's what he'd been smiling about! I'll leave you to draw your own conclusions about the programme being shown again – but I'm sure you know what my interpretation of events would be!

The Christmas of 1970 was a happy one. Unknown to us, life and Christmases would be different from then on. On the morning of January 4th, time for my brothers and sisters to go back to school after the Christmas break, Ken, then aged eleven, woke up with his whole body swollen. He didn't even look like himself.

Mum said he couldn't go to school and made a doctor's appointment for that afternoon. But by the afternoon the mysterious swelling had subsided so she cancelled the appointment. The next morning, though, the swelling had returned and Ken was packed off to the doctor – from where he was dispatched straight to hospital. It was his kidneys. He never came home. He died on Friday February 26th.

Chris and I had been planning a double wedding for March 20th but now I wanted to cancel. However, before I had the chance to say so, Dad decided that we should go ahead as planned because that was what Ken would have wanted. I didn't admit it to dad, I would have been happier not to go through with it. My husband-to-be, though, persuaded me to leave arrangements as they were so as not to upset my father further. He was, after all, grieving for the loss of his son. My father liked my would-be groom – even if I wasn't entirely convinced that I loved him. Nevertheless, my aspiring husband assured me that I would grow to love him one day and that in the meantime he had enough love for two! If I was unsure at the time, I did end up feeling that he was right. Later on I felt much happier about things, as he'd said.

Once again, though, we were all trying to balance feeling happy and sad at the same time. I'd hardly got the hang of this the first time around. But this time it wasn't just pets but my brother who had passed away – something I never quite got over. And I'm sure I'm not the only one who feels that way.

This was the first time that the person who had died actually was from my family; in fact, was from our house. Although I was hurting just as much as everyone else, I felt that I should be brave for Mum, Dad and the rest of the family's benefit. I kept wondering whether I would ever see these missing people again. Part of me always thought that I would. Actually I had seen my grandmother – but thought I'd imagined it because I'd been scared of her and hadn't cried when she died. The second person that I saw from the spirit world is the nurse, on whom I've relied heavily as I've said before. She has always been around in times of trouble and the time of Ken's illness and soon after his passing was no different. His passing changed my life considerable because of the way it affected my family.

My father had often told us as children that he was an atheist. Yet he also told us stories about growing up as a choirboy – as I've said, his mother was very religious and forced God upon him throughout his childhood. This didn't convince him to believe. It had the opposite effect – until my brother fell ill and was clearly dying. Then my father prayed. Since atheists, by definition, don't pray, my father can't have been one. This realisation made me rethink his position – and mine – in an ever-changing world.

My father was a strict man back then and was always in control so I suspect that my brother's death brought about all kinds of new feelings in him. Suddenly he wasn't the master of one of his children's fate and there was nothing he could do about it. He couldn't help and he couldn't begin to put things right,

I've never forgotten an incident when I was about ten that made me aware of just how much my father loved me. Dad never left the house without two clean, starched, freshly ironed hankies – one for show and one for use. One lunchtime on the way home from school, I fell over and grazed my knees so badly they bled.

As I rounded the corner into our road, Dad was coming towards me in the car, on his way to work for the afternoon shift. Seeing that I was upset, he stopped. There was no time to take me home without being late for work so he wrapped one of his handkerchiefs around each of my knees and went on to work without them. This proved to me one hundred percent how much he loved me. My brother's death affected him a great deal. He changed in the way that he reacted to everything and mellowed a great deal. My youngest sister, Ann, who was born after Ken's death would talk about a father who was much gentler, more easygoing than the Dad I'd been used to. It's hard to believe the two are the same. Sometimes it is in situations like this that create problems when a medium is trying to pass on information from a loved one in the spirit world. For example, if my father was giving a message to my youngest sister the medium would feel that he was a strict and strong-minded man. Ann would refute this. This was not her experience of him but it actually described him well. It's not that she lied – both versions are true. Similarly, Chris and I spent most of our time together as children yet we have very different memories of the same Dad. This is just because we're different people with different opinions. In fact Dad favoured me – so I saw him in a different light.

A medium would, therefore, need to tell us different things to jog our memories despite the fact that Dad would be exactly as he always was. I am only saying these things as an illustration of one of the many problems a medium is faced with.

Mum and Dad used to tell us true stories about the times when they lived with my grandmother shortly after they were married. They had one of the upstairs rooms and spent quite a bit of their spare time in there. One day, while they were in bed, they heard a banging noise coming from the wardrobe. They both sat up abruptly, looking at each other, puzzled. When nothing more happened for a few minutes they settled back down and tried to sleep. Then suddenly the whole bed jumped into the air as if someone had given it a powerful kick from beneath. This happened a few more times until Dad lit a candle (Grandmother didn't believe in electricity). Cautiously emerging from the bed he peered underneath it and into the wardrobe but there was nothing and nobody to be seen. The next day they arranged to go and live with my mum's sister!

Being married changed my life as well as those of others. It must have been a difficult time for my parents – first losing a son for what they thought would be eternity and my sister and I both leaving home at the same time. It must have felt as though they'd lost half of their family. For the first two months of married life, my new husband and I stayed with Chris and Derek. My husband was beginning to show signs of violence. I'd have left him then if I'd had somewhere to go. My father's point of view on the subject would have been, 'You've made your bed. Now you can lie on it.' In other words there was to be no going back. Having moved in with my brother and sister-in-law in Tamworth for a further month we became eligible for a council house there.

Moving into our house was very hectic – as these things always are. The stress was exacerbated by the fact that I was pregnant, having been talked out of my desire to put off having children for a while. I worked very hard preparing the house for the new baby. She was due on December 22nd but decided to put in an early appearance after I fell down the stairs with a little help. Born on St Andrew's day, November 30th, Dawn made life seem a whole lot better. Having had her straight away turned out to be a very good decision. That Christmas was a happy one because it was Dawn's first – but at the same time sad because it was the first without Ken. Remembering the happiness of the previous Christmas: how we had no idea of the problems ahead, made the difference hard to deal with. But, of course, we coped.

Our house proved to be haunted – and at that time I didn't

realise that I could do something about it. Nor did I realise that being just nineteen and living with my husband was more of a hindrance than a help, due to the psychic energy I was creating. Whenever my husband walked into the kitchen our small brass ornaments would fly off their shelf opposite the door and hit him. He was afraid to go upstairs alone, convinced that there was someone there. I'd laugh at this, although I had to admit that I often heard footsteps or bangs and that the lights were forever switching themselves on and off.

One day my husband had spent the money he was supposed to have used to pay the electricity bill. Needless to say the first I heard of it was when they came to cut the electricity off. I was very upset. He'd really let us down this time. We went to bed early to keep warm, taking a candle upstairs with us. The candle had been extinguished for about ten minutes when, very cold and upset, I remonstrated with my husband again. How could he have done such a thing when we had a young baby to look after! As usual his response was to shout at me and at that very moment the candle lit up again of its own accord, the bedroom door opened and slammed shut with a bang and the room went suddenly extremely cold. My husband leapt out of bed and tried to open the door. It was stuck fast – so he jumped fearfully back into bed and cowered under the covers. He had nowhere to hide – the covers were whipped right off the bed. The bottom draw of the dressing table repeatedly opened and closed and suddenly an old man appeared, walking across the room holding an old fashioned 'Wee Willie Winkie' style candlestick with a lighted candle. He walked straight through the wall of the fitted wardrobe and, instantly, everything returned to normal. If only I had known that the psychic energy I was producing was allowing all this to happen, perhaps my life would have improved a lot sooner. In other words, I think my husband would have left me there and then!

A few months later, we were sitting in our lounge with the light on when suddenly the bulb blew. Or at least that's what we thought happened. The room had two light sockets – one at each end – but the other bulb had gone the preceding day and we'd removed it. I told my husband to get one of the two bulbs in the hall. But when he stood on a chair to change the bulb in the lounge he found that the socket was empty. 'It must have fallen out. It'll be on the floor,' I said. Once the light was back on we searched the room but couldn't find the bulb. It was a mystery. The next day, while I was doing the housework, I found it at the opposite end of what was a rather long room, in a corner behind the armchair. To have travelled this distance it would have had to bounce several times without breaking. This was surely impossible. But it definitely got there somehow!

CHAPTER 6

Moving into the unknown

From a very early age, Dawn showed signs that she too was aware of those other people about whom I've been writing and, by the time that her sister Toni was born she had become adept at talking away to herself – or rather at communicating with the spirit world. She would often say things that you wouldn't expect of such a young girl. For example, on the Christmas Eve after her first birthday, she was walking alongside me, holding on to the handle of the pushchair, which was full of shopping because I was five months pregnant with Toni and couldn't carry it all. She looked up at me and said, 'Manage, Mum?'

Don't forget that she was not quite thirteen months old at that time! Toni, on the other hand, turned out to be a very naughty child who liked to be held and cried whenever I put her down. She was like this until she was nine months old, when the doctor suggested that I put her in Dawn's room so that she'd have Dawn for company – and wouldn't be disturbed when we went to bed. It worked. Yet on the first night I thought I'd heard her crying and went upstairs and gently opened the door. She wasn't crying. She was laughing at some shadows on the wall, which I assumed were made by Dawn, up on all fours on top of her bed. But when I glanced over at Dawn she was fast asleep. Turning quickly back to the wall, I found that the shadows had gone and that Toni, like Dawn, was fast asleep. She stayed that way until the following morning – as she did every night after that.

When Toni was twenty-one months old a brother joined them. Although due at the end of February, he was born prematurely after a slow, difficult labour on January 16th, 1975. During that arduous confinement I had a memorably frightening experience. Having been given some gas and air by the midwifery nurse I suddenly realised that I was floating up above the bed, close to the ceiling. I could hear the nurse say to my husband, 'Is she normally dumb?' My husband asked her what she meant by this and, in a very agitated voice, she replied, 'Can your wife normally speak?' 'Yes she can,' he replied. At this point she kept patting my face and calling my name repeatedly: 'Jean, Jean…can you hear me? Jean…Jean…'. Having had no response she decided to fetch the doctor. I distinctly remember being bathed in bright light – and being aware that the nurse below me was in a panic. But I wasn't afraid – in fact I felt totally serene. Then I was aware of a voice telling me that the baby needed me and that I must go back – at which I was thrust back into my body. A flush of relief suffused the faces of my doctor and nurse and with that Dean was born. To this day I'm not entirely sure whose voice told me to go back. But I'm ninety-nine percent convinced that it was my brother Ken's. Now that I'm a medium and understand things so much better I think this was Ken taking care of us all from the spirit world.

Dean was very poorly as a baby and we thought we were going to lose him. But thanks to the brilliance of his paediatrician at the local hospital combined, with the excellence of our local GPs, he rallied and got better.

During their childhood, my children occasionally talked about a nurse who walked around their bedrooms at night, making shadows on the wall. She was seen there even more often when any of them were ill. They all remember the nurse today – and all of them are capable of training to become mediums. I hope they'll do so when the time is right.

After many ghostly happenings we moved house back to Sutton Coldfield where I was born. My husband spent more time out of work than in and would only be employed in short spurts – mainly after I'd threatened to leave him if he didn't. He found himself a job in the boiler house of the local hospital. The problem was that he had to work nights one week in three and was afraid of being in the boiler room alone at night. This meant that on each week of nights I had to wait till everyone else there had gone home and sneak into the boiler room to keep him company. While there I often saw a man walking through and stopping as if to stoke the boiler – for which there was no need because it was automatic. My husband, though, couldn't see the man, but only hear him, which frustrated me because I couldn't see how he could be missed. Of course, I didn't realise that he was in spirit.

My husband was petrified. But he had the perfect excuse for walking out of yet another job! Not that he ever really needed an excuse. My children and I took these kind of happenings for granted and thought little about them. Or we didn't until one Sunday morning whilst getting the children ready to go for lunch at Uncle Ernie and Auntie Kay's house. Suddenly a flash of light appeared from nowhere. I didn't know then that this was the first step towards my life changing forever. And I wouldn't realise this for some time yet.

After a delicious Sunday lunch we were all sitting, chatting and laughing as you do in good company, when I said that although we were having a good time it was time we were heading for home. I explained that we'd missed our usual Sunday morning church service and that we ought to get back in time for Evensong (a church service held every Sunday in the Church of England to which I then belonged). My uncle replied, 'Why don't you stay for tea and come to church with us before you go home?'

This was a perfect solution since we were enjoying ourselves too much to want to cut our visit short. The chatter and laughter began again and, after tea, later that afternoon, my aunt said to my uncle, 'Ern', don't you think we ought to tell Jean what sort of church we go to?' To be honest, my immediate thoughts were, 'Oh no. What have I let myself in for?' I need not have worried because my uncle's reply was: 'Oh yes Jean. We go to a Spiritualist church.'

Actually I didn't have any idea what a Spiritualist church was. But I knew it would be all right – partly because my aunt and uncle are very nice, respectable people who wouldn't lead me into anything wrong. I suppose my relaxed attitude was also in part due to an as yet unused inner knowledge of the spiritual world. Of course, I didn't understand this at the time but still replied without a second thought that this was OK with me. That evening we walked into a Spiritualist church for the first time, not knowing what to expect. I was full of apprehension and curiosity but I trusted my aunt and uncle implicitly.

It was a lovely little church in Stirchley, Telford and it was full of really nice people who went out of their way to make us feel welcome. I actually serve that church these days, now that I'm a medium, and my husband and I are lucky enough to be friends of the people who run it. When it was time for the service to start, a lady walked out of the little room at the back onto the rostrum. I was surprised that she was so ordinary, dressed in typical Sunday-best clothes. I'm not sure what I'd expected but it still brings a smile to my face when I hear similar reactions. The lady was introduced as Joan James, the medium for the evening, and the service began. I for one was wrapped up in every word. She was very good and, despite the fact that one of her messages was ostensibly incomprehensible, I recognised every word. Since it was my first time at a service like this I was afraid to put up my hand and say aloud that I thought I understood the message and that it might be for me. Luckily for me, I was able to speak to my uncle about it afterwards and he had a word with the medium, whom he knew. Kindly, she invited me to join her in the little room to which she'd retired for a cup of tea. I was very nervous – but equally curious to hear what she had to say. I recognised most of what she told me straight away – except for one point on which I was sure she was wrong – and told her so. She insisted that she wasn't and I promised to ask my mother about it. It had been a most interesting day and, when I left Telford late that evening, I wasn't aware that my life had changed permanently.

I was tremendously excited and couldn't wait for the next day to arrive so that I could ask my mother about what the medium had told me. When I related every word, including the piece of information that didn't make sense my mother surprised me by pointing out that the message had indeed been correct. The unconvincing part was that Joan told me that there was a young man in the spirit world who must have had a finger missing. This made no sense to me but Joan said, 'Well why does he keep folding his little finger down and holding up his hand as though it were missing?'

Mum reminded me that she used to play a game with us when we were children as well as another that Joan had mentioned which involved making cats cradles with wool on Mum's hands. This other game involved hooking a piece of wool onto her little finger, then through the rest of her fingers. Then she'd pull the wool through her hand, folding down the little finger as she did so – making it look as though it had been chopped off! So Joan had been right after all. I just didn't remember the game until Mum reminded me.

This incident set me thinking – and more deeply than my family realised. It was the subtle beginning of a fundamental change in my life; a change, I'm sad to say, which was to dismay certain people. But that was their problem. Not mine. Thoughts of what that lovely medium had told me tended to blend with those of all the other occurrences I'd experienced over the years. A part of me knew exactly where she had got that information from because I assumed that everyone was just like me; that all people could see, hear and sense these people whose existence I'd always taken for granted. It was to be four more years before I took the next step forward towards my work with the spirit world. Looking back, that's quite surprising – especially when you take into account the excitement I was filled with on that occasion.

I'd always thought that children need their father. But I eventually worked out that staying with my husband didn't protect them – it put them into as much danger as it put me. And the danger was from him. So I made the painful decision to divorce him – I say painful because at the time I objected strongly to divorce. I felt that once you've made your vows you should keep them for life. But the day after he left us for good my daughter, twelve at the time, came in from school, gave me a hug and said, 'Do you realise, Mum, our house is a home again?' I knew then that I'd made the right decision and, although it was a bit of a struggle for the next few years, we were all much happier. My children were – and are – the greatest blessing that I could have to see me through those dark times.

It was quite a shock to the whole family when my father fell ill with cancer and died. Suddenly this strong man who's always been there for us was helplessly ill and needed looking after like a baby. My mum was an absolutely brilliant carer – going far beyond what most would see as duty. We all owe her a great deal for this on top of the monumental task of giving birth to and bringing up nine children. One afternoon while a few of us were visiting my mother our talk turned to the subject of our father, as it often did, just two months after he'd passed to the spirit world. For some reason I couldn't understand or explain I said that I'd like to go to a Spiritualist church but that I would be too scared to go alone. My brother-in-law instantly said that he'd go with me if I found out where there was one. Immediately, the others joined in, saying that they'd like to go too. I didn't need any further encouragement and as soon as I got home I began looking through the telephone directories for a Spiritualist church. Disappointingly, the search was fruitless. But just as I was about to stand up to put the last book away my hand went into spasm – it often does this due to calcium deficiency arising from my Hypoparathyroidism which was caused by the accidental removal of my parathyroids during surgery. This made me drop the book. I reached out to grab it and, as I pulled the open book towards me I noticed that it was open on a page headed: 'Places of Worship'. I'd looked elsewhere but hadn't thought of this heading. On closer inspection I found the name and number of the local Spiritualist church. Still amazed at how I'd found the number I gave it a ring, which was answered by a very nice lady who was the church's President. She kindly explained to me that Monday afternoon would be the best time to visit the church because a very good medium would be taking the service who'd be perfect for beginners to see. I didn't really know what that meant but took her advice. The family was keen to go with me and eight of us set off that Monday in my brother-in-law's new minibus-type van. We were all full of excitement and enthusiasm but it turned out that I'd misheard the name of the road. After some difficulty we finally turned up outside the church – ten minutes late. I said that we couldn't possibly go inside after the start of the service. Perhaps it would be better to come back another time. My brother-in-law, though, wasn't so easily deterred and said they were all going in and that I could wait in the van if I wanted to. That changed my mind and in we went. As we tiptoed through the doors a man emerged from another room (I now know him as Don) so I whispered to him, 'I'm sorry we're late. We got lost. Shall we go away and come back another time?' He just smiled brightly and answered, 'No, it's all right. There are seats at the back...But go in quietly please.' Taking the proffered hymnbooks we walked quietly through to the back of the church and took the remaining seats. As we entered, the medium on the rostrum called out, 'Oh look! A coach party!' Everyone in the room laughed, including us, which made us all feel at ease. The medium then added, 'Maybe now we'll find out why the last message from the spirit world hasn't been understood!' He proceeded to give each of us a message from people who had died. We were all impressed – and I was especially so. If I had gone to the church alone that day, I'd never have gone in because I hate being late for anything. So, who knows, I might never have got involved with spiritualism at all. So I owe a big thank you to my brother-in-law, Ron and of course to Don who made us all feel so welcome that afternoon.

Anyway, I came away keen to find out more. This was to be my second big, important step forward on my spiritual path of discovery and, in the following months I was to learn things of great import, yet with which I was also in some way familiar.

Sadly, many of the ways in which the spirit world communicates with people are misunderstood, so they are passed over or even ignored. This is not because the person receiving the information is necessarily uninterested but because they put it down to imagination or intuition: that questioning, 'Is this me?' This is a fairly common feeling.

During the months that followed I was fortunate enough to meet some very special people who helped me on my may. Because I'd been in touch with the spirits all my life without knowing it I was able to practise sitting for anyone who'd let me – mainly friends and friends of friends. It's important for anyone wanting to develop their spiritual side to practise constantly. Our guides and helpers in the spirit world are like teachers; there to help us with our lessons. And like the teachers at school they won't move on to a new lesson until we've perfected the one we're working on. After all, if a job's worth doing, it's worth doing well – so why not aim to be the best. Bear this in mind while practising your development and your spiritual side will become a natural part of you and everything you do. This means that you as a person and you in your role as a medium will have the fact that you're ordinary etched on your heart and soul. This will ensure that your ego doesn't take over and prevent jealousy of others having any place in your work. Believe it or not, once jealousy of another medium who's doing better than you comes into play, it actually lowers your vibration – so you won't be able to link with spirits as effectively.

In my opinion, this is because we use the top three 'chakras' while linking to the spirit world and the lower ones for negative emotions such as jealousy and hate. 'What are chakras?' you might ask. You can buy books which explain them but for now all you need to know is that we have eight main chakras:

1. The base chakra, which is red in colour and is found at the base of the spine.
2. The sacral plexus, which is orange in colour and is found between the base of the spine and the navel
3. The solar plexus, which is yellow and is found at the navel.
4. The heart chakra, which is green is found in the centre of the chest near the heart
5. The throat chakra, which is blue and found in the throat
6. The brow chakra which is indigo is found at the bridge of the nose
7. The crown chakra, which is violet and found at the crown of your head.
8. Last but by no means least is pure white and situated about a foot above your head.

Chakras are part of the etheric body – not the physical. We

actually use the throat, brow and crown chakras to help put us on the right vibration to be able to see, hear or sense the spirit world around us. This is because we use them for opening our third eye.

Now I'd like to introduce you to another exercise which will help you if you're interested in developing your gift. I call it a gift not because it makes us special but because, like any other talent which we're born with, this needs nurturing. After all, a concert pianist isn't born playing great music but their ability is most definitely there, waiting to be developed and nurtured.

For this exercise you'll need to be in a quiet, semi-dark room or space – I say semi-dark because you need to be able to see the glow of a torch. As well as a torch, you'll need three circular pieces of coloured paper - one blue, one indigo and one violet - at least ten centimetres in diameter.

1. Decide who's going to be A and who's going to be B
2. Sit facing each other about two feet apart.
3. B now holds the blue circle in front of their chest, facing A
4. A now focuses on the blue circle while trying to visualise the colour blue and nothing else
5. B now shines the torch at A's throat, holding the torch above the blue circle which is still held in their other hand
6. A (trying to ignore the torch beam), must concentrate their thoughts on the blue circle while picturing the colour blue being transferred into their throat. In the meantime, B counts slowly to a hundred in their head. On reaching a hundred the torch is switched off.
7. Now B exchanges the blue paper for the indigo.
8. Repeat 4, 5 and 6 as before with the torch beam directed at the bridge of A's nose instead of the throat. A also needs to concentrate on the colour indigo going into their brow chakra, which is just above the bridge of the nose.

9. Now follow the same steps using the violet circle, this time with the torch pointing as close as possible to the centre of the top of A's head.

10. B now holds all three coloured circles together, showing part of each colour. This time the torch needs to be shone / directly onto the three pieces of paper – not onto A

11. A now pictures all three colours blending together to combine into one, stretching from A's throat, through to the brow, through the face to the top of the head.

12. It's now time for A to explain to B everything that has come into their thoughts during the process. This information doesn't have to be connected with the colours or to the experiment itself – although it should be recorded if it is.

13. Finally, repeat the whole process in reverse order. This is purely to allow both A and B to strengthen their abilities.

These exercises should not be rushed. In fact it's probably best to spend as long as you can on them. Repetition is always a good idea if we want our brain to become accustomed to acting out a set of rules which we put into it. After all, it is our brain that we use to link with the spirit world and communicate.

CHAPTER 7

My Guides Working With me

Talking of guides working with me may sound out of context – so I'll explain how these guides work with me and one another to bring through spirit communication. We all have what we call a 'Guardian Angel', who's with us from the moment we are conceived. Mine is, as I've said before, a Russian gentleman. I know him extremely well, having known him all my life. I guess you could say that I'm one of the lucky ones because I do actually know him – unlike most of us who are never aware of our guardian angels. He is, however, just one of several guides. As the leader, he stands just behind my right shoulder, towards the centre while two more guides stand behind him on either side, placed in order of seniority. Behind those two are three more guides – one in between them and one either side. Behind them stand another four guides and behind them another five. To picture this, imagine an inverted triangle with fifteen people inside it rather like the snooker balls set up in the triangle for a snooker game.

These guides work together as a team at all times when I'm linking to the spirit world. Without them I couldn't work as I do. People tend to think that mediums like me call up the dead and assume that this is why we're able to contact the spirits for them when we're doing a sitting or a service. This isn't true.

As soon as an appointment to see a medium has been made,

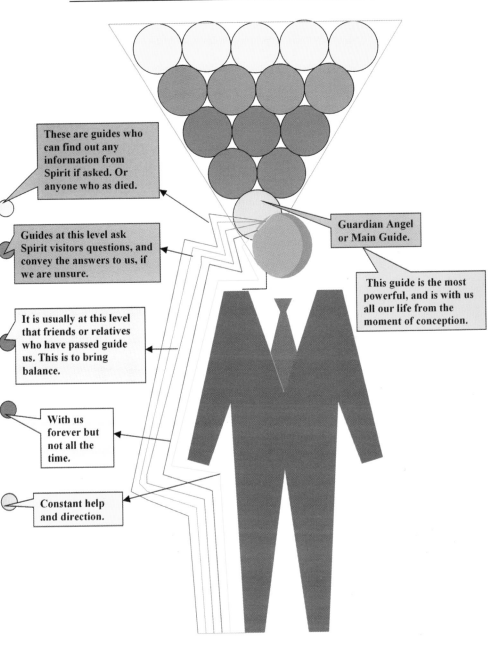

These are guides who can find out any information from Spirit if asked. Or anyone who as died.

Guardian Angel or Main Guide.

Guides at this level ask Spirit visitors questions, and convey the answers to us, if we are unsure.

This guide is the most powerful, and is with us all our life from the moment of conception.

It is usually at this level that friends or relatives who have passed guide us. This is to bring balance.

With us forever but not all the time.

Constant help and direction.

the medium's guides set about their job of contacting people in the spirit world who might want to speak to the people concerned. The guides know exactly who will be attending the service or sitting – sometimes before we know ourselves – so the friends and loved ones of those people can be notified in advance. Whether or not the spirits concerned will get in touch will depend on whether they want to – as well as on a number of other factors. For instance, they might be busy at the specified time, perhaps being with someone else they're close to here on Earth. That other person might need them more than you do at that time. They have a lot of other things to do too – so their non-appearance doesn't mean that they don't love you or wish to visit you. It probably just means that they're too busy or occupied elsewhere for the time being.

Sometimes even mediums' lives become too emotional or difficult for them to be able to function normally – and that's when our guides are really put to the test. A true professional carries on wherever possible because people have made an appointment to meet with their loved ones in the spirit world. The people who've passed on have also made the effort to be there, so if the medium doesn't turn up, he or she has let both sides down.

As you can imagine, it isn't easy in times of trouble to carry on regardless – and that's when we need our guides to come very close to us and take us over. This should make it doubly clear to you that there's nothing special about mediums. They're ordinary people. Like me, in fact – as ordinary as they come and proud of it!

People tend to look at mediums in one of two ways. They either put us on a pedestal, where we don't belong or they keep their distance because they think we're weird. It's a shame they don't grasp that the only reason they feel that way is that we're dealing with the unknown – and that every time part of the subject is explained properly it becomes normal, logical and ordinary. In other words, explanation removes the sense of weirdness or the spectacular.

Shortly after my first trip to the Sutton Coldfield Spiritualist Church, a lady called Margaret asked me if I'd like to go to the Saturday morning Healing Circle, since I was quite poorly at the time. I have to admit that I didn't think much of faith healing (as opposed to Spiritual Healing). I'd been to some very nice healers but they hadn't made me feel any better. Naturally I thought Spiritual Healing would be the same. Nevertheless I liked and respected the lady who'd invited me and thought I'd go along. That Saturday morning I walked into Church and was made very welcome. Although everyone else was sat in a circle to receive healing, I couldn't sit for any length of time because of a chronic back problem – so I was allowed to stand. Margaret and her husband, Hugh, gave me healing and I had to admit that I felt a great deal of peace from it – something I never got from faith healing. That Saturday morning I'd gone along convinced that it couldn't work – and here I was feeling an effect. Better still, when I got out of bed the following morning I was surprised to find that I was feeling slightly better. Some people will say that healing is all about mind over matter – that if you believe it enough you will feel better. Margaret and Hugh are exceptional healers – but I still could hardly believe that I felt better! From that day on I was a constant visitor to their Healing Circle. It did me good, as did going to church in general. On Margaret's advice I also attended the Church's awareness classes and was amazed at how easy I found the exercises. This was a terrific step forward, in that it encouraged my belief that I already possessed the ability to link to the spirits. Margaret gave me a great deal of inspiration and was immensely helpful in my progress towards becoming a medium. A few weeks later I gave my first perfect message to another lady in the class after Sue, the medium taking the class, insisted that I had it in me. We were both very excited by my success and from then on there was no stopping me and I practised and practised on anyone who'd let me.

One Monday afternoon, after attending another service at the church, I arrived home by taxi, being too ill to drive at the time, to find Dawn and Dean in a panic because the house was on fire. My son had put a pie in the oven and forgotten it. The kitchen had caught fire and the fire brigade was on its way. Although the damage was quite bad, it was nothing compared to the one five years previously. The firemen saw to it that Dawn, Dean and I were taken to the hospital in an ambulance because we were suffering from smoke inhalation. They assured me that they would lock the place up safely when they had finished and, while we were gone they put the burnt-out fridge, freezer and oven out in the back yard in case they re-ignited. The floor had been burnt away, the kitchen cupboards were badly scorched, the door leading into the kitchen was half burnt and its glass shattered and everything, everywhere was blackened. My other daughter, Toni, had been away visiting friends but had come home early, arriving before we got home from hospital to find the place in this terrible state. She panicked – assuming that we'd all been killed in the fire – so it must have been far worse for her than for the rest of us! As soon as I phoned to tell them what had happened, Margaret and Hugh came round to help. In fact they were more helpful than they'll ever know because things were about as low for me as they could get. It was their spirituality that saved the day.

Later, when Toni had calmed down, she explained that when she'd first walked into the house the door between the hallway and the lounge was open – which usually meant that someone was at home. She was also sure that she'd heard someone walking about in the kitchen – that is until she entered and found all the mess. Even so, she insisted that she had also felt a breeze wafting through the lounge when she first went in.

I believe that the spirits were keeping an eye open for us that day because Dawn had been asleep and Dean engrossed in the television when the fire broke out. Dawn had been woken up abruptly by what she thought was a nightmare and went into the kitchen for a drink of water – when she, of course, discovered the fire. I also feel that it was spirits in the house when Toni arrived home.

A few weeks later, a couple from the awareness class, Pat and John, asked me if I'd like to go and see Stephen Touroff, the psychic surgeon. They were taking a minibus full of people to see him and since I was poorly, they thought he might be able to help me. I jumped at the chance – and it was on this visit that I was to meet a medium who would ask me to join her circle. After the first week as part of this circle, she decided that she'd like me to help her directly since I linked so well to the spirit world. Some weeks later she asked me to come along and observe her holding a service. The church was a Spiritualist Church in Catshill, Bromsgrove. On arriving, the President came over to say hello and the medium introduced me and said that I'd be on the rostrum with her. The President said that this was OK with her and disappeared to get ready for chairing the service. I turned to my friend and said, 'I can't go on the rostrum with you!' She smiled and replied, 'Well if you don't come on now, you'll make me look a fool because she's gone off to write your name on the chairing details.' Although I was very flustered and nervous I couldn't embarrass her – she meant well, after all.

As it was a clairvoyance service, there was a prayer, which the medium conducted, we sang a hymn and then came time for the messages. After a couple of these, my friend introduced me. As I stood up I was shaking so much that I had to take my high-heeled shoes off to stop me falling over – not that it helped much. I did, however, manage to pass on some messages from the spirit world and to my surprise they could be understood! After the service the Chairperson said to me, 'Now tell me how long you've really been on the rostrum!' I assured her that it was my first time – at which point an elderly gentleman came up and said. 'I could tell it was your first time. Well done!'

I smiled and replied, 'Was it that bad?' He laughed, answering, 'No, it isn't that. It's just that you were shaking so much that when you held on to the front of the rostrum for support, the whole rostrum shook.'

We both laughed at this and I've never forgotten it. And since practice is the most important thing to a training medium I went on to do all the future services with my new friend. Now my progress was in leaps and bounds – for which I owe her another debt of gratitude.

The following Christmas, my friend and I were in the middle of a service – and I was in the middle of a link – when all the lights went out, plunging us into total darkness. Evidently the Christmas tree lights had shorted out the electricity supply. Like a true professional, I decided to carry on in the hope that we'd get the lights back soon. I dragged out the message I was in the process of relaying but soon realised that this was turning it into a private sitting – so I needed to move on to the next link. I couldn't even see the congregation, apart from some vague shadowy figures in the front row, and they couldn't see me either so I asked the spirits for help. On my guides' instruction, I asked whether there was a lady seated one row from the back, next to the wall and described her appearance and clothing. There was no reply so I repeated the description. Again, no answer. 'Have I got that wrong? Is there no one fitting that description in that seat?' I asked. Very quietly came the reply, 'Yes it's me.' 'Thank goodness for that,' I said, 'I thought I'd gone blind and deaf for a minute!' this raised the vibrations because it made everyone laugh and I continued the service. At the end, by which time the lights had been fixed, I was having a cup of coffee when the lady who'd received this message came up to me and explained that it was her first time ever in a Spiritualist church. She added, 'My friend talked me into coming but I was very nervous because another friend told me that you sit and hold hands in the dark. So when the lights went out it scared me. I didn't know what to think! It also shocked me that you knew what I was wearing even though it was too dark to see. Then you shocked me even more by telling me things about my grandfather that I'd never told anyone!'

We laughed at this and I told her not to listen to the rubbish that she'd been told but to judge for herself. I also commented that, 'the only time that I would sit and hold hands in the dark would be with my partner – and I'm sure he wouldn't mind.' This also got a laugh. That lady is a spiritualist to this day and I'm sure that this is a happy memory for everyone who was there that day.

A little later on I was approached by a President of a church who said I'd be the perfect person to take their circle. I was very nervous on that first day – but I couldn't help laughing to myself when one of the ladies walked into the room looking even more nervous than I was. It was Laureece! She told me later that when she'd heard that Jean Kelford would be taking over the circle's teaching, she'd said. 'Oh my God, you're joking! She is good!' that's because she puts herself down too much when actually she's a wonderful person and a great friend to have, as I'd find out later. We often laugh about this now because she's a very down-to-earth person who tells it like it is! It's hard to imagine her having been afraid of me because we're now such good friends that she insults me all the time in her nice, happy-go-lucky way. On that first night we'd been doing an exercise which helps people to see an aura and Laureece saw one for the first time. She was jumping up and down in excitement, lifting her skirt above her knees as she did so and I remember thinking once again, 'Oh no, what have I let myself in for?' It turned out to be the beginning of a very good friendship with lots of laughs along the way. She encouraged me when I was particularly unwell and in our spiritual work. She had a way of always keeping my feet on the ground – in fact that's one of the most important aspects of working with spirits – not getting big-headed. You'd never be able to get big-headed with Laureece around to keep you grounded – something else I'm grateful to her for.

A few months later, once that particular circle had come to an end and we'd had a break, Laureece and Annie, another friend I'd met at the same circle, began sitting together to help the two of them progress. One evening, we were sitting in Laureece's bedroom because downstairs was too busy with all her family, when all of a sudden I saw someone from the spirit world swinging a belt that was hanging over the wardrobe door. The belt was nowhere near where we were sitting so it couldn't have been knocked. There were no windows or doors open to admit a draught, yet it was swinging away all by itself. I pointed this out to the other two and they both screamed and ran, jumping up and down, across the room. You have to bear in mind that I could see the spirit person but they couldn't. All they could see was the belt swinging away vigorously apparently of its own accord. I think all three of us will remember this occasion with a smile.

On another occasion we were at Annie's place doing a lesson on overshadowing. This is when someone from the spirit world comes up very close to the medium and overshadows them so that the medium takes on the features of the spirit. I was allowing the spirits to overshadow me so that the girls could see how it was done when I noticed that tears were pouring down Annie's cheeks. I quickly asked the spirit to step back and asked Annie what was the matter. She wiped her eyes and explained that her mother from the spirit world had overshadowed me and I had looked just like her. I apologised at once, saying, 'I didn't mean to upset you – I'm sorry,' She was smiling now as she replied, 'I'm not upset – I'm happy. It just surprised me a bit.'

This taught me a valuable lesson – that sometimes people cry because they are both surprised and pleased at the same time. This is likely to happen a lot when we are linking someone here with people whom they love but no longer see or hear from because they have passed over.

Eleven years after divorcing a man who had made my life a misery, I found myself remarrying. I never thought I'd marry again having had such a bad time with my former husband but the spirits and circumstances had other ideas! One day, over coffee in her garden, my friend Pauline (Polly to her friends) asked me to get my diary. For some time now we'd been planning to go for a curry together and she'd decided to set the date. We arranged to go on a Wednesday evening in a fortnight's time. The Sunday before our curry night I wasn't on the rostrum, so I decided to go and see Polly because she was working at a church in Harbourne (she's another good working medium!). The lady with whom I usually worked decided to go with me. When the service was over, Polly asked me if we were still OK for Wednesday. I said yes and that I was looking forward to it and, since my other friend seemed left out, we invited her along as well. Wednesday night came around and I picked up my friend and headed off to Polly's. When we arrived, Polly said we'd have to wait a moment because her brother was coming with us. Straight away, the spirits said to me, 'She's matchmaking.' Although this made me nervous, it also made me smile and we sat down to wait for Polly's brother to arrive. Minutes later the doorbell rang and Polly went to answer it, returning a minute later with her brother. I have to admit that I thought to myself, 'He's a bit of all right! I don't mind her matchmaking if he doesn't!' She told us that his name was Mick and, on her suggestion, they went in Mick's car while we followed in mine. Once seated in the restaurant according to Polly's instructions – which meant that she was opposite my friend and next to her brother, and that I was facing him – she said, 'Right Jean, this is my lovely brother Micky. He's wonderful and free and single. And Micky, this is my lovely friend Jean. She's also wonderful and free and single.' We both went very red but hit it off straight away. In fact we didn't stop talking all through the meal while the two ladies chatted among themselves. Needless to say, Micky – or Mike as he preferred to be called – and I started seeing each other and I was pleased to find out that he had thought the same thing as I had on our first meeting.

A few months later I was on cloud nine when Mike asked me to marry him. Of course, I said yes right away. There were a few problems though. Mike's youngest daughter, Jenny, wasn't too sure about us being together. In fact she hated the idea at first. She'd sit on the sofa and glare at us. Being a bit of a 'Daddy's Girl' – mainly because she was ill with cystic fibrosis – she didn't want him to go out with anyone. One evening I arrived at Mike's flat while he was still in the shower, getting ready for our evening at his work's Christmas dinner. Suddenly Jenny said to me, 'Why is it that I like you even though I don't want to?' Taken aback, I asked her why she didn't want to like me. Her answer surprised me even more because she said, 'Because you are going to steal my Dad away and go to live abroad.' Now puzzled as well as surprised, I said, 'What makes you think that we'll go to live abroad?'

She looked at me for a moment before replying,

'Auntie Pauline told dad that he would meet someone who has grown-up children still living with her and that they would marry and go to live abroad.'

Now it was making a bit more sense. She obviously thought that since the spirits had been right so far the rest was bound to come true. I gave her a reassuring smile and said, 'Well, if I promise you that while you're alive, even if you live to be a hundred, we'll never go and live abroad, how would you feel about that?' this seemed to please her:

'Do you promise? Because you wouldn't break a promise!' she said. I made that promise right away and from then on we were friends. In the spirit world, they had decided that it was important that they change Mike's way of thinking about the existence of life after death. I should explain that Mike did not believe. In fact, when we first started going out together I'd gone straight to his flat after doing a service and was talking about the spirits when he interrupted, 'Jean, I should tell you that I love Polly to bits but I think she's a loony! I don't believe in all that!' This surprised me, but my answer was, 'That's OK, as long as you realise that it is what I do. I enjoy it, people say that I'm good at it and it allows me to help people so I'm not stopping. If you agree with that, I won't mention the spirits to you any more unless you ask me to.'

He agreed and we changed the subject. A few weeks later, though, I arrived at Mike's flat one night and Mike asked, 'How's your work with the spirit world going?' Shocked, I answered, 'OK. In fact your Mum's here now.'

This seemed to ruffle him a bit but he replied, 'Is she. What does she want?'

Typically for me, I replied, 'I don't know – I haven't asked her. I've been working with the spirits and I'm here to rest!'

'You mean she's not really here!' was his immediate riposte. Before I had the chance to say anything the two lounge doors and the bathroom door swung open and the room was scoured by a blast of wind, which scattered papers everywhere. Mike's face said it all. But he spoke anyway, saying, 'All right, I believe you!' The doors slammed shut again and the wind died down. I should explain that the doors in Mike's flat were fire security doors with sprung hinges that made them very difficult to open. In fact my inability to open them had become something of a standing joke among our friends – although it was as much to do with my health problems as their resistance. Mike actually had to let me out of the room, they were so hard to open – so we joked that they were his cunning little 'sex trap'! Any way you look at it, though, those doors would have needed more than a stiff breeze to fling them open! Yet the spirit world had opened them as easily as a knife going through soft butter. The incident had made Mike think but it wasn't till later that the spirit world would conclusively prove its existence to him.

One evening, whilst we were visiting Polly, I asked Jenny to be our bridesmaid. She wasn't keen on being a bridesmaid in general but said that since it was I who'd asked she would be happy to. Mike joked, 'I think that Dean should pay for our wedding because he's doing your father's bit in giving you away, he might as well finish the job!' As you'll have gathered, I'd asked Dean to give me away since Dad was already in the spirit world. There was a family joke associated with this request – the joke being that my Dean spends money as fast as he gets it. He'll give you anything if he's got it – but you'd have to be quick because most of the time he hasn't two halfpennies to rub together! Nevertheless, my answer to Mike's jokey comment was, 'If you want my father to pay for the wedding, he's in spirit – why don't you ask him!' Suddenly both Polly and I heard my dad say, 'Why do you think I sent you the lottery?'

We were taken aback by this because although our wedding had been planned for the following year, Mike had said that he'd like to bring it forward – Jenny was going through a bad patch and we didn't know how she'd be feeling by that time. That Saturday, I'd been booked for a service at Kings Heath Church. By this time, at his own request after the incident with the spirit in his flat, Mike came with me sometimes to watch me working. On the way to the church I asked Mike to stop so that I could go and place my lottery numbers but, having stopped at the shops, I couldn't find the checklist with our numbers but there wasn't time to hang about if we were to get to the church on time. Just as we were about to give up on the lottery and go the ticket caught my eye and I asked Mike to go and pay for that number combination. After church, when we checked the numbers we couldn't believe our luck – we had five numbers and won £695. That may have been the lowest five number pay-out that year but it was enough for us to be able to bring the wedding forward to October 11th that year!

So you see, my dad had helped to pay for the wedding after all! It was also appropriate because our wedding was to be a beautiful ceremony at Kings Heath Church. Although Don, the Church President, had never conducted one before he gave us a first class ceremony. Even my elderly aunt who was reluctant to come to a Spiritualist church for a wedding said that it was the best wedding service that she'd ever attended.

When Mike moved into my place he was a bit worried by the strange, inexplicable things that kept happening. For instance, hearing footsteps creak across the landing after we'd been in bed for ten minutes or so when there was no one else in the house. This bothered him to start with and when the bedroom door handle went down and the door burst open he'd go white as a sheet. Of course I'd tell him not to worry, saying 'It's only spirits.' Mike preferred not to believe that it was spirits because that represented the unknown of which he was still a little afraid. I was used to my guide doing this and knew that he was merely looking after me. This reminds me of an occasion a few months earlier when only my son and I were in the house. We were both in bed when there was a noise downstairs. Our bedroom doors were at opposite ends of the stairwell and we both arrived on the landing at the same time. I said in a whisper, 'Please God, let it be spirits!'

On hearing this, my son replied, 'Please God, let it be a burglar!'

This was because he was more scared of the spirit world than he was of burglars because he felt that with a burglar he could see what he was up against. With spirits, however, it was a completely unknown quantity. I, on the other hand, was sure that the spirit world wouldn't hurt me – but knew that a burglar might. So I felt safer hoping that it was someone from the spirit world!

For Mike, the above incident was just the start because the spirit world had decided that it was time for him to accept that it really did exist. One night, about five minutes after we'd gone to bed, there was a bang on the bedroom door – so loud that it rattled the door on its hinges. Mike went whiter than usual and my answer was, as usual, 'Don't worry, it's only spirit.' Unfortunately Mike didn't seem very reassured by this.

Each night for the next two weeks the same thing happened. One night, Mike said thoughtfully, 'Jean, do you realise that the door only knocks when you close it. If I'm the last one in and I shut the door, it doesn't happen.'

This surprised me. 'Are you sure? That is strange,' I replied.

We decided to test this theory. For two consecutive nights Mike closed the door and nothing happened. Then, when I took over door closing duties the knocking and rattling started again. After giving this some thought I decided to find out exactly who in the spirit world was doing the knocking – a fairly simple task for a medium. I determined that from the moment I went into the bedroom that night I would not take my eyes off the door. I'm sure you're wondering how that helps if the knocking is coming from the other side! The answer's simple. If the medium is quick enough in sending out their senses they can find out who's there even if they can't see them. An experienced medium can also tell whether a person they can hear in another room is dead or alive.

That night, as planned, I didn't take my eyes off the door for about fifteen minutes. It seemed as though nothing was going to happen and I turned to mike and began, 'It isn't going to.....'

I was interrupted by the knock at the door. Mike shivered from head to foot. I swivelled to find two young ladies from the spirit world standing by the door. I asked who they were and one of them answered, 'We're friends of Jenny. We also had cystic fibrosis and passed to spirit last year. We know him as well.'

As she said this, she pointed at Mike. I asked her what she wanted and she replied, 'We want you to help Jenny and her dad to believe in the spirit world because Jenny will join us here soon and it will be easier for both of them if they believe.'

This made sense, but I couldn't see how I was going to achieve such a difficult task. I thought for a moment and then asked, 'Can you tell me something to tell Jenny – something that her dad doesn't know about because if her dad knows she'll say that he told me.'

Her immediate response was, 'Tell her that while I was alive we were in hospital together one time and the nurses let us have music on in the television room after the visitors were gone. We used to lock the door and have a sort of party. One night Jenny and I sneaked out of the hospital and across the road to the off-licence to buy some beer. On the way back, we were messing about in the lift when a security guard caught us and took us to the Staff Nurse in charge of the ward. Because we were so upset, she agreed not to tell our parents as long as we promised not to do it again. We never told anyone.'

The following day, when I relayed this story to Jenny, she was amazed and had to agree that the only place from which I could have got this was her friend in the spirit world. This was the start of her belief in life after death. In fact her affectionate, laughing new nickname for me was 'Mrs Know It All'. Proving that the spirits existed to Jenny turned out to be a lot easier than proving it to her dad – in fact the spirits had to pull out all the stops to convince him. Although not finally convincing him, the incident with Jen's friends had certainly made him think – he had actually sensed their presence in the room before they knocked on the door. That was why he'd started shivering before they appeared!

CHAPTER 8

Proof of a physical kind

Sadly, Jenny was taken to the spirit side of life on Saturday August 9th, 1997. She suffered a great deal in those last days and I'll never forget when she said, about two weeks before her passing, 'Jean, will I go home?'

'Yes, of course you will,' I replied with a reassuring smile. At the time I knew that she meant home to the house where she had lived with her sister Karen and brother-in-law James. This was a place in which she'd been happy. Although I knew that this was not going to happen, I also knew that once in the spirit world, she would realise that she was, in fact, home. So I hadn't lied – just been economical with the truth for her own benefit, for which I'm sure she'll forgive me.

However, the night before she passed away she became lucid for the last time and told us all that she loved us. This included me so, you see, I had been accepted, having kept my promise not to live abroad while she was still alive. Suddenly, Jenny lifted her head up so that she was half-sitting up. Looking towards the foot of the bed, she said. 'Who's she?'

Jenny's grandmother – Mike's mum – who is in the spirit world was standing by the foot of the bed. She had come to meet her. Jenny did know her grandmother but was obviously seeing her in a mist as is quite normal in the circumstances. Mike and I knew that her presence meant that it was almost time for Jen to go.

Two hours had gone by since Jenny had finally let go of her hold on life and passed to the spirit world. Mike and I were back at home and I went up to the toilet, where Jenny suddenly appeared in front of me.

'Hello Jen, are you all right?' I responded without hesitation.

'Yes, Jean. But will you tell my dad,' she replied and with that put both arms in the air and floated up through the ceiling. 'Strange girl!' I thought. But I did go straight downstairs to tell her dad. He was very surprised but said that he knew straight away what she meant. He went on to explain that when she was a little younger he'd taken her two sisters, Karen and Faye, abroad on holiday. The doctors would not let Jenny go with them because the pressure differences during the flight would be bad for her chest. She was naturally upset and said, 'Oh Dad, I wish I could fly.' Obviously she was now saying to her dad, 'Look Dad, I can fly!'

Although this pleased Mike, it was still just intellectual evidence of the spirit world's existence. He needed something more physical.

Time went by and we were married on the date we'd set and although we missed Jenny, we knew that she'd be there. Everything went well and Mike and I went away for a week in a borrowed caravan in Wales, feeling that we needed a quiet week together after all the traumatic events of recent months. The caravan, incidentally, belonged to the mother of Chris, Polly's partner. Chris has now passed to Spirit and his mother joined him there two months later. They are both sadly missed but, I'm sure, happy where they are.

When we arrived home, Toni showed us the photographs that she had taken at the wedding. Among them was one that Mike had taken of Toni with her then fiancé Paul and my niece Mikaela. Just above them on the wall was a clear picture of Jenny's face. You could clearly see her hairline and her eyes through her glasses. This was the evidence Mike needed that Jenny definitely had been at the wedding – which obviously pleased us both immensely. A few days later we noticed that a picture of Jenny and her boyfriend Andy, which hung on our lounge wall, was crooked. When I pointed this out to Mike, he said, 'Someone must have knocked it.' The following day a photograph of Mike and I, which hung on a wall behind a sideboard, was also crooked.

'It's impossible for someone to have knocked that isn't it?' I said. Mike thought for a moment and replied, 'There must be something wrong with the picture hook.'

I didn't reply because he'd already made up his mind. He was presenting the spirit world with quite a challenge – but one it's more than capable of meeting!

As we go to bed every night, Mike makes the drinks and carries them upstairs – it's not safe for me to do so because of the spasms that seize me from time to time. I switch the main light on and the lamps off while he's making the drinks and then I switch off the main light as we leave the room together to go upstairs. On this occasion our routine played itself out as usual until we got up the next morning to find that all the lights were on. Mike's immediate conclusion was that we must have forgotten to switch them off. I disagreed – but to no avail. The next morning, however, Mike was to get a shock that he couldn't so easily explain. When we came downstairs the exceptionally heavy sideboard had been moved a good foot or so away from the wall. Mike knew that I couldn't have moved it – he could only just shift it himself. He also knew that he was a light sleeper and would have been aware of it if I'd got out of bed for anything more unusual than a trip to the bathroom. This time he put his hands in the air and said, 'All right, spirits, I believe you!'

From then on, the noises and movements quietened down considerably. The spirits knew that they'd made their point. Now that Mike had been convinced that there was a spirit world he began to look at things differently. This was a great help to me because we were now working towards the same aim rather than pulling against each other. We were travelling home from a church service one evening, when Mike said, 'Jean, can I ask you something?'

I was driving at the time so I just gave him a quick smile and said, 'Of course you can. What is it?'

He hesitated a little before saying, 'Will you teach me?'

'Teach you what,' I asked, puzzled.

'To link to spirit of course,' he replied with a smile.

I must admit that I was completely shocked by this – in fact I'm amazed that I didn't crash the car. Anyway I told him that I'd be happy to teach him and Mike's training began – all thanks to the spirits' activities in our house.

At this point in my life I began asking the spirit world lots of questions. They always seem ready to answer – if not always straightaway. For me, it is important that things have some sort of logic to them – and I'm a firm believer that if you can do something you can teach it.

You need to find a common sense, ordinary way to tell people about your subject so that they too can understand its logic. This is what I set about doing next. I asked Izeakial how the spirits link to us and he explained that it is by using our brain's. That's when he gave me the instructions for this workshop, which is a good one for trainees to follow.(see next page)

At first view this exercise might look quite difficult – but don't

Jean Kelford.

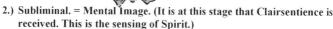

1.) Guardian Angel.

2.) Subliminal. = Mental Image. (It is at this stage that Clairsentience is received. This is the sensing of Spirit.)

 3.) Reflective. (At this stage our brain starts to reflect an image of what we are sensing. For example we can sense how tall the person is from this image.)

4.) Comparison. = Subjective Image. (Our brain now makes a comparison of what we are sensing through this image, this allows us to see a form that is likened to a photograph negative.)

5.) Individuality. = Third Eye. (Spirit stimulates our third eye at this point, in readiness to see the image, or images.)

6.) Perceptive. (Our brain now tries to perceive what information it is picking up.)

7.) Reflective. = Objective Image. (We are once again back at the reflective part of our brain, the chain is complete and an objective image can be seen. An objective image appears solid like you or I.)

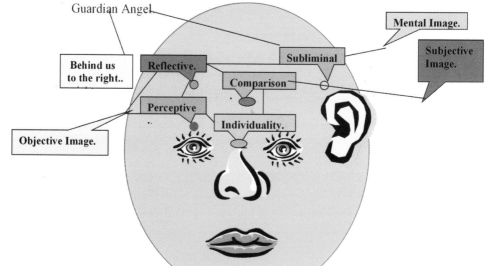

Brief Description Of How Spirit Use Our Brain To Communicate.

give up because it's easy once you get used to it! As I've already explained, our Guardian Angel stands behind our right shoulder in order to be in the best position in which to work with us during our communication. The very first part of the brain that spirits need to connect with for sensing. To begin is the subliminal part. This is situated just above and forward of the left ear. All mediums use this part of the brain because all mediums sense spirits whilst linking– whether by seeing, hearing or feeling them or, like me, using all three.

At the first stage of linking we may get a thought into our head – for instance, the name:

'Tom'

This on its own isn't much because all sorts of questions then pop into the medium's head. And of course most of us could find a Tom somewhere in our lives, past or present. So this alone wouldn't stand up as evidence.

Then we might ask:

'Is Tom dead or alive?'

Good question! But one which would be difficult to answer at this stage if you didn't know what you were doing. One of the first things that the would-be medium needs to learn is the difference between a thought and a subliminal message because, as I've said before, the golden rule is do not think while you link. As soon you begin to think you might change the whole message; thereby making a true message appear to be false. The only difference between the two concepts is that a thought is solid and takes time to form whereas a subliminal message is lighter and appears very quickly. It is only with practise that we can learn to tell the difference. It is also useful to know that a thought tends to stay with you and a subliminal message does not.

Now say, for instance that you have learnt to tell the difference and you know that the spirits have indicated the name Tom. The next question has to be:

'Is Tom talking to me or am I just being told the name Tom?'

This is very important because if you say, 'I have got Tom here.' And it turns out that Tom is still alive and well you've got it wrong. However, if you say instead:

'They are talking about a Tom?'

This is a little better but it still doesn't establish for sure whether the Tom in question is here or there. Because you are only getting a sense, rather than a concrete thought, it is important to make sure that you have made a note of all the information available to you. If you are more aware of being back in the place in which you were standing when you received Tom's name, then he's alive. If, however, you are more aware of the spirit side, Tom is in the spirit world. Remember that you are only sure that the man you are talking to in spirit is Tom if he says so. This is because even though you're certain that Tom's in the spirit world you could be talking through an intermediary in the spirit world. If you then take the connection further into your brain you will begin to use the reflective part of your brain, which is situated on the opposite side of your head. This should help you to see a clear mental picture of anything that the spirit world wants you to know about. I should point out that it won't always be the picture you expected to see. So don't be tempted to say what you had expected instead of what you are actually seeing. This, again, would change the information and make the message wrong – despite the fact that the spirit world has tried to communicate something correct. I say that you should get a clear picture – in fact it sometimes looks like a photographic negative. You might say that's not exactly clear – but if you think about it, a negative contains just as much information, just as accurately as the finished print. To extend the metaphor, the difference between the two mental pictures is that the 'print' is easy for our eyes to see properly. The 'negative' on the other hand requires us to use an invisible eye, which is brought forward by love. In other words, if we care enough to pay proper attention we can see just as much, if not more, on a negative as we can on the finished photograph. Love and attention are all you need – and don't forget that the spirits are providing most of that love!

I'd like you to close your eyes for a moment and picture a beautiful golden stairwell stretched out in front of you. At the top are the people you love most and who have gone on to the spirit side of life ahead of you. They are walking down those stairs smiling brightly. There are about thirty stairs and they have quickly descended twenty-seven of them in anticipation of talking to you. However, having reached that far, they find that the bottom three steps are missing and they can't finish their journey to you. All they're asking you to do is think of them with as much love as you can so that the three missing steps appear and you can connect. Their love was, after all, strong enough for them to negotiate the first twenty-seven steps so it's not a lot to ask for you to return enough love for the last three.

The next stage of our brain which is used while linking to the spirit world is the comparison part which is roughly in the centre of the head, on the edge of the left hand side. Assuming that you have already decided from the information you've received that Tom is in the spirit world it is now time to work out whether the person you're communicating with is Tom himself. To do this you must sense this person in comparison with yourself. Are you sure that it is a man? If, like me, you're female, you will soon learn that a man senses differently to a woman. Make that decision first:

'Yes. It is a man.'

Ask yourself:

'Is he taller or shorter than I am?

You might conclude that:

'He is slightly taller.'

91

Remember that since you know your own height, so you now have an approximate idea of this man's height. I am five feet three and a half inches tall and this man feels as though he is about four or five inches taller. He is, therefore, about five feet eight inches tall.

The next question to ask yourself is:

'Is he fatter or slimmer or about the same size as me?'

You might then conclude that he is slimmer in the body, except for the fact that his stomach is bigger. Now it is time to find out:

'Does this person have more or less hair than I do?'

He has less – in fact not much at all. So I hope that you are beginning to see how much you can find out just by comparing them with yourself . We have found out that the man visiting us from the spirit world is a slimmish man who is a bit rotund around the middle and is about five foot eight inches tall with a fair amount of hair loss. Already we are beginning to build up a picture of the person to whom we are speaking. Now is the time to ask inwardly:

'Did Tom look like this?'

You would be surprised how, at this point, if you're not communicating with Tom, you'll be aware of another person, even if only for a moment. You now know whether or not you're talking to Tom. This information can all be gained in a matter of seconds and I assure you that as soon as you say one thing the person concerned will make you aware of the next. So the trick is to start talking and don't stop! After you have established all the information that you can from this point – which gives you a subjective 'negative film' image – it is time to use your brain's 'individuality' area, which is situated by the bridge of your nose. At this stage more complex information can be brought into play – referring to things you understand simply because of who you are. For example, if you are a mathematician you might receive mathematical information. If on the other hand you had a bit of a mental block about maths, there wouldn't be any point in the spirits trying to pass you information you wouldn't understand. Similarly, if you come from a large family, spirits would know that you understand the issues involved in large families.

One of the problems at this stage of linking with the spirit world is the way in which it is misunderstood. There is a particular part of the brain, just above the right eye, that's essential in comprehending the information we receive. The trouble is that we don't make that connection and therefore don't fully understand what we're being told.

However, having already stimulated the third eye (which is just above the bridge of your nose), you have reached the stage where you can see the spirits objectively – especially if you look at things laterally using the reflective part of your brain again. Seeing spirits objectively is like seeing them as solid entities just like you would see people or objects. It's very important to use your brain in the right way – hence the importance of brain-stimulating exercises to our spiritual training. The workshop shown a few pages back will help in this – but it's no good on its own! You'll need to practise what it suggests and meditate while you're doing so!

There is an exercise which may help when first starting out with stimulating different sections of your brain and that may help you to practise starting and stopping at different parts of the way. This is important in order to understand what you are feeling and why. You'll find it better to work with a group – it teaches you discipline as well as giving you more people to practise on. As before, you need to meditate, running slowly through the links with the brain as shown in the workshop on how to use our brain.

At first you'll find you can only pass on the information you

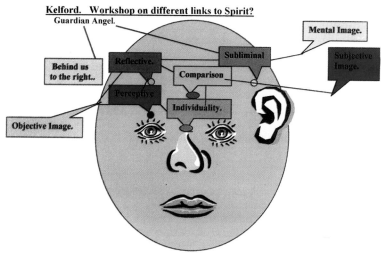

Brief Description Of How Spirit Use Our Brain To Communicate.

The class split into three groups, dependant on what colour stone they have got? Pink, Blue, or Green? This is done leaving a gap between each team? We now have a blue team, a green team and a pink team, who are separate from each other.

A meditation takes place, making links through the brain. As the part of the brain is reached that your group colour covers, the leader will say, for instance, the blue team will stop listening now and concentrate on what Spirit are trying to communicate to them? It is at this point that communication with the Spirit world should take place?

The leader then brings the class back and asks them to sit together? Now asking each one in turn what colour bead they have, which is purely to allow them to know, who their message is for? This is defined by who has the bead of the same colour. After the first persons partner has been defined, they are then asked to give each other their message?

The leader explains things as they go along giving help where it is needed?

After which this is repeated with each couple until all have given their message?

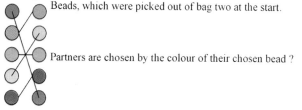

Beads, which were picked out of bag two at the start.

Partners are chosen by the colour of their chosen bead ?

It is always with amazement that the people realise, that the person can understand their message from the Spirit world? This usually comes about because during this exercise they do not have time to think whilst they link?

received during the meditation but eventually you should be able to link on further, giving information as you speak. Practice is the only way to build your confidence in yourself and your spiritual work.

Teaching Mike to link with people on the spirit side of life proved to be a pleasure. He started off just sitting in on our sittings without saying anything. But soon he'd occasionally interject the odd piece of information and, if the person who was having the sitting didn't understand, I'd tell him to go back for clarification. Of course, I'd always let the person concerned know that if they were still baffled at the end of the sitting by anything Mike had told them I'd sort it out for them! People always thought I was rather cruel when I kept repeating, 'OK, go back and get some more.' In fact I was being cruel to be kind, as they say – and the upshot was that I never had to sort it out for him!

One such incident in particular sticks in both of our minds. While doing a sitting, Mike told the lady in question that he was aware of an old man who kept putting his head up a chimney. He had nothing else to mention but a pocket watch and a few other items such as money…that kind of thing. Losing confidence, his commentary tailed off into the admission that: 'I know this sounds mad – I must be getting it wrong!'

The lady laughed and explained that he wasn't mad at all. In fact he was quite right. When her grandfather died his wife and family couldn't find his things. They searched and searched until one day her grandmother remembered that he was always messing about up the chimneybreast - being unused, the hearth was never hot. Acting immediately on this vital piece of information they looked up the chimney and found his secret hidey-hole – a loose brick, behind which was revealed grandfather's pocket watch, cash and a number of other sundry items. So you see, you should never discount what you're told, no matter how silly it sounds, because the spirit world always have a good reason for bringing a piece of information through. It usually makes sense to the person receiving the sitting very quickly. Next to 'Is it me or spirit?' I believe one of the hardest things to learn has to be:

'Is this person whom spirits are telling me about dead or alive?'

Once again, this takes a lot of practice. Don't forget, though, what I said earlier – you can learn to sense whether they are with you in the here and now or in spirit. For people like Mike who mainly sense the spirit world it is slightly harder because they only see a picture within their mind rather than a spirit person standing in the room they're in.

One day, a lady was referred to me by someone at the local hospital. All I knew about her was that either she had just lost someone close to her or they were dying of cancer at the time. But I wasn't told how that person was related to her or where the cancer was.

On the Monday morning of the week in which I was due to see her I noticed that I had put her name in the diary twice – on two consecutive days. I had never made this mistake before – yet when I looked for her telephone number so that I could check which was the correct entry I found that I'd made another mistake. I'd neglected to take her number! And she lived about an hour's drive away. Again, this was the kind of mistake I never made.

I thought about the problem and discussed it with my husband. We decided that we'd have to go to see her on the first night and, if it turned out that she was expecting us the following night, we'd just have to do the trip all over again! So we set off that evening hoping we'd got the right night – if not it was a considerable waste of time and fuel! An hour later, we pulled up outside the address we'd been given.

I looked towards the house and could see a lady standing in

the window crying and fiddling with something in her hand. I was a bit apprehensive knocking on the door, not being sure whether I was supposed to be there or not. The lady I'd seen in the window answered the door looking a little surprised.

'Yes? Can I help you?' she enquired.

Now I knew we had the wrong day – because surely she'd have guessed who we were if she'd been expecting us. So I smiled and replied, 'we're Jean and Michael Kelford. We're mediums and we have an appointment with you.

Her puzzled look said it all, but anyway she answered, 'It's not today. It's next month!' This really surprised us – we were half expecting to be a day early but not a month!

'Are you sure?' I replied, 'we had the appointment written down twice, which is unusual – in fact it never happens. But we have nothing in the diary for this time next month. This never happens!'

'Yes, look I'll fetch my letter from the hospital,' she said, looking slightly flustered as she walked off towards the kitchen. Sure enough the letter gave that day's date but for the following month. I apologised for the mix-up and said we'd return next month. But she said that since we were there, we might as well do the sitting now.

Her young son had died recently after suffering with bone cancer and she was delighted when he came through with a lot of information about himself, his mum and dad and other family members. She told us that the session had helped her a great deal and added, 'Can I tell you something?'

'Of course you can – anything,' I replied without hesitation. She smiled a beautiful smile that made you feel sad that she had so little reason to smile at the time.

'You know when you arrived tonight?'

'Yes. You were in the window,' I replied, smiling reassuringly. She smiled again and began, hesitantly:

'I had a bottle of pills in my hand and I had just said out loud to my son, "if it is possible for you to hear me and you do not want me to kill myself to be with you, then give me a sign." At that precise moment, your car pulled up outside and you have given me some beautiful proof that my son is all right. And I take this to be his sign because of the misunderstanding about the date. You arrived at exactly the right moment to save my life – thank you both very much!'

Both Mike and I felt very humble as I explained to her that she shouldn't thank us but her son in the spirit world for answering her prayer in a way which she could not doubt. Then I added, 'He wants you to carry on with your life and be as happy as you can because he loves you and does not want to be responsible for making you unhappy. Please try for him. You will never forget him or stop missing him but I promise you that with time the sadness that you feel now will be anaesthetised. When that happens you will be able to carry on with your life, safe in the knowledge that one day you will meet him again and you will all be together.'

I don't think we'll ever forget that day. You'd think that when you link to spirit every day like we do, they wouldn't be able to surprise you any more. Just when you start thinking this, they come up with something like this, totally out of the blue. And to say that they shock us is probably the biggest understatement that we'll ever make.

During that same sitting, Mike described a man in the spirit world who had a beard, rode a bike and worked for the railway. The lady and her husband, who had since arrived home, tried very hard to place him and could not – until I said to Mike, 'Are you sure he's in the spirit world?'

Before he could answer, the lady's husband said, 'We can think of a man like that – my uncle. But he's still alive!'

'Has he been off-colour recently,' I asked, 'because they are sending him healing.'

He seemed quite excited by this because his uncle had only told him that morning that he was feeling unwell. We all laughed about the fact that Mike had put his uncle in the spirit world before his time. I explained that he should have known he was still alive by the way that he was presented to Mike; that is, as being in the here and now. This was the last time Mike told any-one that someone was dead when in fact they were still alive!

CHAPTER 9.

Learning to let go

After Jenny had been in the spirit world for almost a year, she realised what a bad state her Dad was in. As I mentioned before, her face appeared in one of our wedding photographs – which was a giant step forward for Mike into believing that there's no death and that Jenny really is all right. Unfortunately, Toni had the photos and they were in her car when it was stolen. Sadly, when the car was finally recovered, the photos were gone. Mike was so upset about losing this picture of Jenny; this proof that she was still alive, that he had a nervous breakdown.

Quite often, when the face of someone who is in spirit appears on a photograph, it doesn't show up when you take another print from the same negative. On this occasion, though, it did! Not quite as clear as before, but perfectly discernible all the same.

The week before the first anniversary of Jenny's death, on the Sunday morning, Mike was pottering about the garden in a world of his own as usual (I wasn't allowed to do anything because I'd only just come out of hospital.)

The previous week we were in bed, asleep, when the bed

broke. It's a pine one with slats across it and it fell apart because Mike obviously hadn't put it back together properly last time he'd dismantled and moved it. You have to bear in mind here that I'm not in the best of health to begin with – and this latest disaster caused me to rupture a muscle in my groin that connects to the spine. I could hardly move with the pain and, after spending a week in hospital, I was ordered to rest with my leg up on a stool – and that's what I was doing in the garden that August Sunday morning when, suddenly, Jenny appeared in front of me.

'Jean, will you write this poem down and read it to Dad?' she said.

Of course, I said yes but that she'd have to wait while I asked her dad to get me a pad and some paper. He did so and, as she recited the poem, I scribbled it down as quickly as I could. This done, I read it to Mike and we both cried. I'd been writing so quickly that there was no time to take in what she was saying – so I was just as taken aback by its contents when I read it aloud. The poem, entitled 'Love Me for Myself' has since been read out all over this country and abroad since Jenny communicated it to me on August 2nd 1998. It has helped a lot of people – so here it is.

Love Me for Myself

To speak of our love is an easy thing,
And to act it, up to a fashion,
But to give your love, or your love bring
Takes the thing we call compassion.

When people leave us because they die,
It appears they leave us for good,
At times like this, the question is why?
For we can't understand why they should.

The love we give to this person then,
Is a love that can never die,
But please don't steal that love from the living,
When we both know it will make them cry.

If you take this love from the living,
You should get it into your head,
The love which you are giving,
Already belongs to the dead.

This means that I must move away,
With a heart that is heavy and sad,
For if you really love me,
It couldn't possibly bring anything bad.

There are all kinds of love in the world as a whole,
But the main one is this,
The light of vibration eternity,
Which is the best kind of spiritual kiss.

If you should lose someone you need,
And you loved them whilst they were here,
Do the right thing to help them with speed,
To depart with their only fear.

This is my worry, that I've stolen your heart,

That you think you can love me only,

Yet from the moment that we were apart.

I truly was never lonely.

All I need to cope, and move on with giving,

Is to see you do the same here on Earth,

That your actions do not hurt the living,

In order to give me rebirth.

For if you really miss me,

You would not need to think all the time,

But to love and be happy with someone,

Whilst keeping my love in the back of your mind.

If I cannot get you to do this,

Spirit must stop my visits to you,

So please help me to visit with bliss,

Then I will know that your love is true.

I suffered enough in my life Dad,

Don't make me suffer in death as your excuse,

Please give your love to others freely,

I don't need you to be a recluse.

My love will always surround you,

So live your life to the full,
If you treat someone else unkindly,
It will make my memory dull.

One year Dad, is not very long,
But for me it has been great,
Please don't treat it all as wrong,
Just live your life and celebrate.

Please do what I ask Dad, just for me,
So that I will never need to go away,
Love and live life normally,
For without this, I just cannot stay.

This poem turned Mike's state of mind around.

'Jean, I will never be sad for her again. She is the happiest that she has ever been, isn't she!' he said, after a good cry.

'Yes love.' I answered simply, giving him a hug.

One of the hardest things for us to do is to let someone we love go when they've passed over to the spirit world. This doesn't mean that you can't think about them any more – in fact quite the opposite. You should think of them and talk to them every day. By talk to them, I don't mean speaking out loud because that's not necessary. They communicate with telepathy (reading the mind) – as mediums do when they pass messages to you from the spirits. The spirits can read every thought – they know when you are thinking about them and why!

I should say at this point that mediums only read the minds of people in the spirit world – not those of people here. It's a good idea to try to sense whether spirits are near at hand whilst exercising to open our third eye. Once you have trained yourself to open your third eye properly you will also pick up an image of the person with whom you're communicating. As I've said before, your third eye is found just above the bridge of your nose.

Try the following exercise regularly – do it sitting down or lying down, with your eyes closed and pretending to be cross-eyed. In other words, look at the bridge of your nose with both eyes while relaxing with eyes closed. At first, most people find that although it is dark (because their eyes are shut), they can see a patch of fog or dim light within the darkness around the bridge of their nose where they're concentrating their vision. This is because they are seeing the glow of the bright lights that shine out of the spirit world. While I'm linking to spirits from the rostrum, I can only see the person in the congregation for whom I'm linking and the spirits. Everything else is in a light blue mist and that is all I can see.

Jean Kelford.   Workshop On Opening The Third Eye?

Close your eyes and picture three discs central to your face as in the picture below.
These discs are in an inverted triangle.
The disc over the mouth is Blue.
The disc over the right eye is Indigo.
The disc over the left eye is violet.
Now picture all three discs are spinning clockwise. However, you need to remember
that because they are within you they are in reverse order.
To make this easy, imagine these discs spinning in the direction of your left ear.
Or imagine a clock covering your face with the dial facing outwards with its fingers
working normally.
As they spin they will create a vortex of energy in the small triangle in the centre of
these discs. This is caused by friction as the three discs rub together where they
connect to each other.
Now try to picture the small central triangle. This will stimulate your third eye
because the part of your brain that controls it will be gently stimulated.
This will in time cause your third eye to operate effectively.

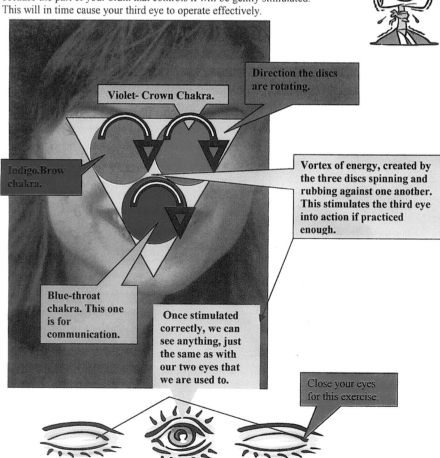

Direction the discs are rotating.

Violet- Crown Chakra.

Indigo.Brow chakra.

Vortex of energy, created by the three discs spinning and rubbing against one another. This stimulates the third eye into action if practiced enough.

Blue-throat chakra. This one is for communication.

Once stimulated correctly, we can see anything, just the same as with our two eyes that we are used to.

Close your eyes for this exercise.

<u>**Jean Kelford.**</u>   <u>**Workshop On Linking, Using The Third Eye? .**</u>

This exercise may achieve better results if a red light is used.

Everyone sits facing another person, and one person at each end of the group facing inwards.

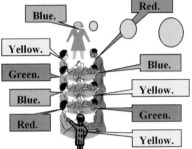

Blue.

Red.

Yellow.

Green.

Blue.

Red.

Blue.

Yellow.

Green.

Yellow.

Everyone is given a coloured bead, by the person in charge. This determines the colour that they need to draw towards them.

First of all we close our eyes and follow a meditation to open our third eye. This is done following the principle shown below.

Discs spin clockwise creating a vortex of air in the centre which stimulates the third eye.

Vortex of air.

Everyone now opens their eyes and looks at the person opposite, at the same time concentrating their eyes towards the bridge of their nose, this will also stimulate their third eye.

They now must think of the colours being used in the group. For example, in the group above, the colours are Red, Blue, Yellow, and Green, therefore, they must think about these four colours.

Next we close our eyes again, asking Spirit where the colour is, that is the same as the one we are holding. Sometimes there is a flash of colour leading to that person, or they may just be drawn to someone, or if they are lucky they will be told a name. Everybody now knows who they think their message is for, therefore they should all close their eyes again for a short meditation on stimulating the third eye by picturing their Guide gently massaging the bridge of their nose. They will then be left for a moment to gain any information they see, hear, or sense, from the Spirit world.

On opening their eyes everyone should be observant of anything they might see, hear, or sense, to add to their communication. It is now time for everyone to exchange messages, but, of cause they must be aware that the two people at the ends of the group, have duplicate colours to someone within the group, therefore, may have a message from their loved ones in Spirit, this could create a cross link?

The vortex of energy mentioned in the last exercise is what created that blue haze. If everything else around you is in a mist so that you can't see it, you'll concentrate much more effectively on the things that you can see. It's just like when you're driving a car in the fog. You concentrate on what's in front of you to avoid hitting anything because you can't see anything else.

People often apologise for a noise or disturbance during a service. But the truth is that when you're linked properly with the spirit world you don't see or hear anything else. You're only aware of this mist, the person with whom you're speaking and the people in spirit.

One evening while I was doing a service with an excellent psychic artist called Sue Wood, a close friend of mine and her friend arrived late after getting lost. I was in the middle of a link when they came in and, although they had to walk right down the aisle in front of me, I didn't see them. It was only as I stopped between links that I noticed her sitting there.

Whenever I talk to my family about the spirit world and my previous knowledge of it, they realise why certain things happened in my past. My brother Keith always makes me laugh when the subject comes up. He'll tell me all about an incident that's happened to him in connection with someone who is in spirit and I tell him, 'I'm not surprised that you can do it. Mediumistic ability is in the genes!'

'I know, Sis'. That's why I don't wear them!' is always his reply. It's just fear of the unknown – so I just laugh it off!

Jenny was obviously very pleased with the response to her poem – after all it helped a lot of other people as well as her dad. She asked me if I'd write down a second poem which would also help other people. Of course, I was delighted to – and here it is:

Don't Be Afraid of Dying

I lie here in the shadow, where all around is dark,
Dying is a time set for the lonely,
I try to think back to being a child in the park,
Of each little memory that is homely.

The fear looms heavy in my mind,
The fear of life's rejection,
Of being in a world of a different kind,
With totally no protection.

The people all around my bed are not sure how to act,
Each one lost in their own world of shock,
They look at me, then at each other, searching for some tact,
Knowing soon I will die and their world will begin to rock.

At that moment, a light shines through, a sunshine to my heart,
With it I relax with peace,
I knew then, love was in my being, every part,
So the fear began to cease.

There is Nan and Grand'dad, Aunt and Uncle, in fact all the
  living dead,
For at this moment, they are more alive than me,
The fear and darkness gone away, now light and happiness
  instead,

In place of being lonely, there are many friends to see.

I have moved across to another stage of my existence,
I am alive, I am alert, and pain-free once again,
So now, I wonder why I offered such resistance,
When now my life's so full of sunshine, free of rain.

If only you people left behind, could see what I can see,
If only your feelings were like mine,
You would be glad to know that at last I am free,
And no longer a prisoner of your time.

I will come to visit every day,
To ease your pain and sorrow,
As I come just like a golden ray,
My happiness, you can borrow.

Each time you accept that I am here,
That I have not gone away,
You will have taken another step near,
To seeing me one day.

Death isn't for the lonely, death isn't for the sad,
It is for those who need some peace.
If you feel lonely or you feel sad,
Remember my happiness will cease.

Let me come near to your heart,

Please let our souls be one,

Then you will know this is the start,

Of all our fears being gone.

This poem was obviously trying to explain how it feels to be the person who has died instead of the person left behind – the point of view we usually see. It has helped many to cope with the loss of their loved ones. That's what mediumship's all about and, of course, trying to demonstrate that there is no death; that we survive death to carry on our lives in a world free from pain and suffering.

I have spiritualism to thank for having met two very special people in my life: Grace and Su. I met this mother and daughter one day when they were part of the congregation for one of my nervous early appearances on the rostrum. Grace looked up at me and beamed a beautiful smile at me – she could see how nervous I was, and that the link I was bringing through at the time was making me very emotional. Her smile helped me a great deal. I'll always remember it as one of those acts of kindness that can take you forward in life. It certainly did that for me! It was a very special act from a very special lady who always smiles from the inside.

The love that she gave to a stranger that afternoon was, and is, exactly the kind of love the spirits need to connect with us. I'm very happy that this stranger became a friend. Su has also become an invaluable friend and is now well on her way to becoming a brilliant medium. She says that she wants to be as good as me. I hope with all my heart that she becomes a lot better because the spirit world needs good mediums and I have every faith that Su will continue developing her links with the spirits in the very special way that she has begun. Susan Bragg is definitely a name for people to look out for in the future!

She has come on in leaps and bounds since the day I suggested that she join my development class. I thought she'd make a very good medium but she wasn't so sure:

'Because I have had a lot of sittings from you and you have never been wrong I trust you – but I think you're wrong this time!'

I corrected her, pointing out that it wasn't me that was always right. It was the spirits. Without them I wouldn't be able to tell her, or anybody else, anything! I also assured her that they were not wrong this time. Since she couldn't link at all when she first started the class she is actually doing exceptionally well. She is already practising sittings on her friends and anyone else who will let her, just as I had done in my early days! In fact she will be making her debut this November (2001) at one of the churches with Mike and I!

This came about when Su's plan to get Mike on the rostrum backfired. One Sunday recently, Su and another student friend called Caroline came to church with us to observe my work. The two girls went into the church to save seats for themselves and Mike in the congregation. Su was chatting to the booking secretary, telling her that she should try getting Mike up on the rostrum because he's very good. She said this because the preceding year, while staying with friends in Newtown, Wales, I took the service at the local church and Kay, our hostess, suggested that Mike went up on the rostrum. He refused at first – despite the fact that he's a brilliant medium in his own right these days. He's quite happy to give sittings to anyone in private but, like all of us, he's still intimidated by the exposure of the rostrum.

'Why don't you just go and sit on the rostrum to see what it feels like? You don't have to actually do anything.' said Kay.

'All right then – but I'm not going to do anything,' Mike replied with conviction.

'That's what he thinks!' interjected Izeakial.

Obviously I was the only one to hear this last comment – so I just smiled to myself. Once we came to the part of the service that called on the medium to give proof of survival I gave some of the evidence and then turned to Mike.

'Have you got anything?' I enquired. Mike met my eyes, went red and said, 'Yes – I'll have a go.'

He got up and gave messages from the spirit world to three people from the congregation – all of which were understood and taken on board. I was so proud of him! The next weekend, in Belfast, he turned to me and said, 'You do the morning service and I'll see if they're aggressive. If not, I'll do the evening service with you.'

The morning service went really well – so he agreed that he was on in the evening one. I should explain that some congregations are more difficult to work with than others – Mike was just checking that these people weren't going to be difficult deliberately. That does happen sometimes!

Tragically, Mike suffered a heart attack that very afternoon and ended up in hospital instead of on the rostrum. He hasn't been on a rostrum since. Su had asked the booking secretary not to repeat to us her suggestion that Mike mounted the rostrum – but she did. Mike's response was, 'She can talk – she's very good herself…She should go up.'

The booking secretary turned to me and gave permission for them both to go up with me. I said that it wasn't fair to expect them both to do so at such short notice. Could they instead come up the next time I was due at the church, in November. She agreed – but Mike panicked and said he wouldn't.

'OK then – can I bring Su and another student?' I answered.

'OK, I'll do it,' Mike exclaimed before she could reply.

'You're booked!' came her swift response. I had no idea why he'd changed his mind – so I asked him.

'If Su got onto the rostrum before me I'd never live it down!' he chuckled. I joined the laughter but Su wasn't quite so confident when she found out. In the end, though, she did agree to pluck up her courage and go on like a true professional!

CHAPTER *10*

Ghostly experiences

One of the things I like most about being a medium is that you can help people even if your health's not too good – like mine. Clearing ghosts scares many people but it's just part of everyday life for Mike and I. If there's a problem with ghost activity we're happy to go along and try to solve it. What a lot of people don't understand is that ghost activity is generally created by a spirit who's got lost and failed to make the transition to the spirit side of life as they were supposed to.

One of my most memorable ghost-clearing experiences was when we were called into one of the very well known food stores. The freezers were repeatedly unplugged, even though the sockets were very difficult to reach and took a lot of effort to pull out. In fact to remove the plugs you'd have to lie stretched out across the top of the freezer and strain to get your arm down behind it. It was deliberately this difficult to ensure that playful children or awkward customers couldn't whip them out and let the food defrost. So there was no question of them having been unplugged accidentally. Despite all this, several plugs would get pulled out even when the shop was closed and therefore empty.

The staff repeatedly tidied up one of the storerooms only to find that food and drink had been strewn all over the floor almost the moment their backs had been turned. One young lady who worked there was stacking shelves when she heard footsteps approaching along the corridor and the sound of someone whistling. Before she had time to investigate, the storeroom door slammed shut and she heard the key turn in the lock. Shouting, she ran towards the door but was too late. It was locked. She was terrified. She was alone in the building. Who could have locked the door? She never got an answer – but two hours later she heard the same whistling again and suddenly found that the door was unlocked. On further investigation, she found that there was still no one in the building.

The manager didn't believe it was a ghost because he hadn't personally seen or heard anything. But when the staff began admitting that they were scared and talking about leaving unless something was done he called in a priest to exorcise the putative ghost to keep them happy. If anything, the fact that they were frightened was making matters worse. The manager turned up the morning after the priest's visit and, as he reached out to switch on the light in the staff room, a stereo unit on the table lifted into the air and hurtled towards him, hitting him squarely on the head. Understandably, this frightened him. He had to admit that something strange was going on and he agreed that the young lady should seek help from a medium. So she went to a local Spiritualist church to ask for help and they gave her my name. Shortly afterwards, Mike and I went along to investigate and asked these spirit souls (and I must say, there were a few of them) to go towards the light (this would take them home where they belonged). We were able to give names and other information about the spirits who'd been there to the staff and, after some research, they found it all to be correct.

This particular store, like many others, employed a lot of teenagers and younger people – and because young people emit so much psychic energy, ghost activity is easily triggered when they're around. Sometimes ghosts haunt a place quietly for years before anyone hears anything from them. Their presence usually becomes apparent because of a younger influence or a lot of tension from illness or arguments continually hanging in the air. Having solved their particular problem, the store asked us back to give a talk to the staff about spiritualism and, of course, life after death. We did this with pleasure and, I'm glad to say, we managed to convert quite a few of them to the idea that the spirit world really exists and that it's nothing to worry about. They also took on board the fact that spirits are often sorely misunderstood because of people's reaction to their fear of the unknown.

Although I said we solved the problem, we did have to pay the store another visit. They kept finding the doors open even though there was no sign of a break-in, there was no one about and the alarms didn't go off. Stranger still, when they closed the doors and then opened them to check, the alarms would be set off instantly. It's important to note that once a ghost had been cleared it does not come back unless invited back. So it wasn't any of the ghosts we'd asked to leave. However, as I said, there were several spirits in the store when we first visited. Ghosts don't haunt people – they haunt a particular space. And this space had been bombed during the war. Many died here – and they died very suddenly. Which is why they didn't realise that they were dead – in short, why they were ghosts, haunting the place where their lives ended so abruptly.

The store had recently employed a new influx of teenagers to complement their staff and, during our first visit we hadn't checked the area around the doors in question. Unknown to me, Mike had had a word with Jenny at that time.

'We're going ghost hunting, Jen. You can come if you want to,' he'd said.

These days, when you see Jenny in spirit you often also see her sister Catherine, who had gone to spirit before she was born, and our friend Claire who had passed to the spirit world after suffering from cancer. This is because we'd asked Catherine to take care of Jenny when she passed over and we'd asked them both to look after Claire when she passed over. They regularly make us laugh with their antics and we've named them the Three Musketeers. That particular day, though, they excelled themselves.

Mike and I were walking through the store with the young lady in charge when suddenly I got distracted. I found myself walking in a completely different direction from the others. Mike called me back, asking where I thought I was going and I couldn't help laughing. I'd been distracted because I'd looked round to see Jenny, Catherine and Claire floating above the fridges, holding one another's hands, arms outstretched, singing the 'Ghostbusters' theme tune. This really made me laugh – especially because they don't need to float! They were just taking the mickey because they knew that the others couldn't see them and I could.

Apparently the staff were also getting 'the spooks' in one of the offices where they'd experience an icy cold sensation. We went up to the office concerned and Mike said he could feel something down by his legs on his side of the office. I asked him to swap places with me and, sure enough, there was a definite sensation coming from the vicinity of a particularly huge desk. Then, the spirits made me aware that there was something hidden behind the desk, by the wall. I asked if this was possible but the answer was no it wasn't. So, on the instruction of a man in the spirit world, I asked, 'Are there telephone wires behind there? And have they been repaired recently?'

'Yes. The repairmen came yesterday,' came the reply from one of them, a shocked expression on her face. I had to smile because you never quite get used to the way they look at you when you tell them something that they think you couldn't know. They were standing there, mouths agape.

'Are the wires behind the desk?' I asked. They all looked unsure but concluded that they must be – so I continued, 'well how do you get to them?'

At this point the young lady moved the only part of the desk that was loose. It was a fitted desk, running right along the wall so that when you looked underneath you couldn't see the wall – just the desk's back panel. However, a small cabinet was free standing underneath it. As she moved it aside I could see what looked like small hinges attached to its back. I asked her what they were. She didn't know – but she crawled underneath to investigate. Sure enough, there was a little door which opened to reveal lots of computer and telephone wires.

'Can you look behind, on the side where I'm standing?' I asked her.

Oh my God I don't believe it!' she exclaimed as she did this, pulling back in astonishment. We were all enthralled.

'Believe what? What have you found?' I blurted.

Without another word she pulled out a large toy hippopotamus wearing pyjamas. Turning to us excitedly she said, 'We've looked everywhere for this. One of the boys hid it up in the ceiling for a joke and when he went back it had gone – no one could find it!'

I asked to whom it had belonged and they introduced me to a young lady who'd brought the toy into work. It had once belonged to her grandmother who had recently gone senile and become scared of it. Her mother had told her that if she wanted to keep it she should take it to work – presumably so that it was out of her poor grandmother's way. But the lads had been teasing her about him – and that's when their little prank happened and subsequently the hippo went missing.

As she spoke, the elderly gentleman who had told me where to look in the first place, reappeared and said that he was her grand-father and was a bit put out about the lads larking about with his wife's once-treasured toy. He also didn't like to see his grand-daughter upset. The incident certainly gave a few of those lads something to think about!

In the process we also made some new friends, including one young lady who was also to become a student with a promising career as a medium ahead of her. Her name was Caroline.

Another memorable ghost-clearing occasion arose when a strictly Catholic lady who was very wary of mediums asked us to visit her house. She sounded petrified when she first phoned me, having been given my number 'once again' by one of the spiritu-alist churches. I tried to reassure her and arranged a visit.

'Ooh you are ordinary!', she said, looking at us strangely as she opened the door.

'Yes,' I said, 'Aren't we what you expected?'

She didn't answer.

'You'd better come in. Would you like a cup of tea or coffee?' she said hurriedly as she motioned towards the hallway behind her. I've never been known to turn down a cup of coffee – and anyway, what better way to show her that we're ordinary people and get her to relax in our company! She was an exceptionally nice lady – she went into great detail about her recent loss of her brother to the spirit world with cancer. She told us almost every detail about him and his family in fact. At least she began to set-tle down a bit once we began telling her all about spiritualism and exactly what we do. The phone rang and she excused herself to answer it. Pleasantries out of the way, she answered the caller, 'No, I'm OK. They're very nice. We're having a cup of coffee before they look upstairs.'

Once she came off the phone she explained that her son had called to check that she was OK because he knew she was alone with us. We laughed and assured her again that she was quite safe but that it was time to get on with the job at hand. We asked what problems she'd been having.

'You'll probably think I'm silly but...' she said tentatively.

We stopped her right there – telling her that everyone thought this but that we were well used to it, we understood and didn't think she was silly at all. She smiled and went on to explain that she thought there might be a ghost in the house.

'Sometimes there is a logical explanation for things,' I said, 'and it's important that we search for that at first. So I need to know what sort of things are happening.'

She went on to say that her daughter's bed covers would lift up and that the mattress would go down as if someone had sat on the bed. Then her daughter would feel someone cuddle up behind her – and sometimes she'd be held down on the bed so that she couldn't get up or breath properly.

'I can understand how frightening that would be for her. ' I said, 'May I ask how old she is?'

'Almost twenty-one,' she said with surprise, 'but it has happened to me too. When my husband goes to work in the mornings the same thing happens to me. But it never happens whilst my husband's here. Are we going mad?'

I assured her that they weren't and went upstairs to investigate. Once in her daughter's room I was aware of a young spirit girl immediately. On speaking to this untidy, urchin-like girl she told me that her name was Amy. Quite a coincidence! She was a little nervous of Mike but told me that she loved the cupboard in the corner of the room because she loved teddy bears – yet had never owned one herself. I repeated this to the lady of the house she looked very surprised and said, 'But if you were to open that cupboard door you'd find it full of cuddly toys!'

The cupboard she meant was a fitted wardrobe with a very

121

tightly closed full-length door – it would be impossible to know what was in there. Amy then explained that she had been run down by a horse while running away from a man who had been horrible to her and of whom she was scared. This didn't make much sense, except in that her wariness of Mike suggested that she was still afraid of men. When I repeated this information to the lady of the house it all fell into place when she said that the house had been built on an old horse racing circuit. Amy couldn't climb into the lady's bed while her husband was around because she was afraid of men. So she'd snuggle up with her daughter and waited until the father went to work and then climbed in bed with the mother. They'd assumed that because it only happened to the women of the house it must be the ghost of a man, when if fact it was something so much more innocent – just a little girl longing to be loved.

The lady of the house now needed to know more.

'Now that I know a bit more about it and know that it is safe, I wish you could tell me something so that I'd know that my brother is all right, ' she said, wistfully.

Right away, her brother appeared in front of me.

'She has told me most things about you already, 'I said to him, 'so if you want her to know you are safe and here to see her, you'll have to tell me something that she hasn't already said.'

'Tell her I've got my sense of humour back,' he said after a couple of seconds.

We were standing side by side by the bed as I repeated to her, 'Your brother has asked me to tell you that he has got his sense of humour back.'

She stretched out her arm, grabbing for my hand, as she fell back onto the bed with tears cascading down her cheeks.

''Are you all right?' I asked.

She smiled the biggest smile I'd seen her give all evening – and she hadn't been short on smiles!

'Yes. I'm happy now that I know he's all right.'

I told her I still didn't understand.

'My brother had a brilliant sense of humour,' she explained, 'and you could always make him laugh...tell him any joke and he'd laugh. But one day, while he was ill, I told him a joke on the phone and he just said, "That's good. I will put my wife on." As soon as she spoke to me I told her that I knew that he was really ill because he had lost his sense of humour!'

This one sentence wouldn't have meant anything to most people but to her it meant the world. It was all the proof she needed. Needless to say we became friends and I'd like to think that she'll never be afraid of spirits or mediums again. I did ask, by the way, whether her daughter had been poorly because Amy seemed to think she had. She told me that her daughter suffered badly with epilepsy. I asked whether she'd been stressed or anxious lately and she replied, 'Yes, she's afraid that she won't get the job she wants because of her fits.'

I assured her that this would not be the case and that it was this anxiety and illness that had brought about enough psychic energy for them to be aware of Amy. She had, after all, been there since the house was built – but no one was ever aware of her until recently. I also went on to explain that quite often people think that spirits are pinning them down onto their bed, when in fact it's just that in their anxiousness to communicate with us they come in too close. This affects our breathing and magnetises our aura too much, which makes us respond exactly like a pin would when it's attracted to a magnet.

To stop this, you only need to relax and ask the spirit to step back a little bit because they are too close. We are in charge of our own bodies – the spirit world is not and they must abide by those rules. For these people, the problem was solved – although the lady of the house did need to call us once more because Amy kept reappearing. I explained that they don't usually come back unless they've been invited and she said, 'Well the only thing that's happened is that my daughter has bought a mobile for her bedroom ceiling and, as she hung it up she said "Here you are then Amy – if you're here you can chime the mobile and let me know." Does that count?'

Mike and I laughed as we both answered together: YES! She's invited her back!'

We laughed and chatted and she decided that it was all right for Amy to visit as long as she didn't scare them by being too noisy. Mike and I left things as they were and presumably things are going OK because we haven't been called back since!

I've already spoken about a young lady called Claire who we were lucky enough to call a friend and who passed to the spirit side of life with cancer. Our meeting was definitely helped by the spirits – Mike had told Su during a sitting that she would go to America and I added that it would happen unexpectedly. A few months later Su heard from her friend Claire in America. She had cancer and Su was very worried. She asked me if I'd make a tape for Claire – and whether I thought she ought to go to the States to be with her. I said that I thought she should – and of course that I'd be happy to make a tape so that she could take it with her.

While Su was away she kept in touch and updated us on Claire's progress regularly – once she even called from the US at two in the morning their time! Another time, at Claire's request, Su rang to say Claire was very unwell and thought that her time had come. I told Su to assure her that it wasn't time yet and told her how to bring healing and peace to make her feel better. Claire said that she was keen to meet me and I told Su to tell her that she would – which she doubted, unless I was able to go to America.

'You'll come to England and meet me,' I replied.

She really thought that I'd lost the plot. After all, she was too ill to travel. But I insisted that I was right. Two days later, Su rang and very excitedly announced, 'Jean, guess what! Claire is feeling a bit better and the doctor has told her that if she wants to go home to England, now's the time. It could be her last chance. We fly home tomorrow!' We were all very excited and were lucky enough to meet Claire twice – once at her parents' home (they're lovely people) and the second time at Su's, where we gave Claire a sitting. During the sitting, Claire said that her one regret was that she hadn't been able to work for the spirit world. I told her that she would, which pleased her immensely. And now she does work for the spirit world in a way that wouldn't have been possible whilst she was in this world – so her wish has come true!

Claire was, and is, one of the most beautiful people that I've ever met – both on the inside and out. She is a credit to her mum, dad, family and friends and it makes my heart swell with pride to see her so happy in the spirit world because I know her and am lucky enough to call her a friend.

CHAPTER 11

Some of the things that made me proud to be a Medium

Being a medium has some very exciting and memorable moments – but it also has some funny ones that we'll never forget.

At one of my services I started to say something:

'Can I...' At which point the Chairperson tugged the back of my jacket and whispered, 'Can you make this a quickie please?'

'Can I give that gentleman a quickie please', I said, smiling as I turned back to the congregation. The whole place went up in a roar of laughter. I didn't know what they were laughing at.

'I don't mind if you don't!' said the gentleman in question and suddenly I realised what I'd said! I went very red and laughed along with everyone else.

Another funny, but embarrassing, one was while I was giving a young girl a message, which I thought she could accept without any problem. I asked her if she understood the date of someone's passing and she became quite flustered.

'I'm sorry, I don't know. I'm not very good with dates,' she stuttered.

'Don't worry. I can never remember the dates of my passings,' I said, smiling in an attempt to ease her nerves.

'Are you dead?' she said, her mouth dropping open in awe.

Needless to say, she'd misheard me because of her nerves and thought that I'd said, 'Don't worry, I can never remember the date of my passing.'

It's on occasions like this that you realise how worrying it can be to be a newcomer to spiritualism. Sometimes we can be just as innocent ourselves when it comes to surprise links. One Sunday evening I was about to start the service at a church in Kidderminster when I was suddenly aware of a lady from the spirit world sitting in a chair next to me. She had brought her own chair and looked completely at home – in fact probably more at home than I looked!

'Who are you?' I asked.

'Don't you know me dearie?' She smiled.

'No. Should I?' I replied with some surprise.

'I'm Doris Stokes.' Came the reply, which knocked me for six as you can imagine!

Then the service started and I had no time to think but afterwards quite a few people said that they thought that I had worked differently that day. When I told them why, they were surprised but said that in their opinion the service had been better than usual. Considering that these people rated me highly, it proved that they were of the same opinion as me. Some might think I'm saying this because Doris is without doubt a deservedly big name and a brilliant medium (I say is, not was, because she's now working just as hard for the spirit world from the other side). People may think I'm hanging onto her shirt tails as it were – but those who know me well and are used to the way I work will agree that there has been a definite improvement since she has worked with me. I feel very honoured by this – and I couldn't write this book without mentioning her tremendous help and inspiration.

One Sunday evening whilst Mike was driving us home on the M42 from a church service, I was suddenly aware of Doris sitting on the back seat.

'You'll be going there soon,' she said with a smile.

'Going where?' I answered, confused.

'Look at the sign,' she said, pointing upwards. I looked at the sign – it said London. I excitedly told Mike – I'd never been to London and thought it would be great to see it. I thought, though, that she meant I'd be going there to work on the rostrum – but it wasn't to be. The following week Toni collapsed in London whilst visiting friends and we had to rush down to London to see her. Toni is doing well now but she needed major surgery at the time and, once again, after she was sent to a hospital nearer home for the surgery she was lucky enough to get an extremely good surgeon. Clearly, I had broken my own very important rule - do not think while you link! – thereby misunderstanding the prediction that I'd be going to London.

It's occasions like this that make you aware how close to us the spirits really are, bringing us their help in the ways we least expect, and when we least expect it.

I was talking on the phone to my close friend Tess the other day when she asked me if I knew whether her father-in-law had been around.

'Yes – he asked me a couple of days ago to ask you what was the matter with the skipping rope.' I replied immediately.

'Oh my God,' she replied, 'as we speak, Amy is outside playing with it. I can see her through the window. But last week she asked me if she could take Dennis's skipping rope to school because all her friends took theirs. I told her that she could as long as she looked after it because it used to belong to her grand-dad. She promised that she would and said that she'd put it straight back into her school bag as soon as she'd finished playing with it so that it wouldn't get stolen. Anyway, yesterday, when she came home she was a little upset.'

'Why?' I enquired.

'I asked the little dude what was the matter and she looked at me a little uncertainly as she said, "I did look after it Mum but a boy at school pulled it too hard and broke the handle a bit." I put my arm around her and asked her to show me the rope. The rope had come away from the handle a bit – although I did manage to push it back into place. I told her that she couldn't take it to school any more because it had belonged to her grand-dad and was of sentimental value and therefore important.'

She went on to explain that her father-in-law had used the skipping rope to build up his muscles to help him walk better on his prosthetic legs. I should explain, by the way, that Tess's daughter coincidentally shares the name of my young friend Amy in the spirit world, although Tess also calls her 'my little dude'.

I first heard of Tess's father-in-law when I was doing a service to raise money for Cancer Research at one of the local spiritualist churches. I gave a message from the spirit world to a lady in the congregation and afterwards she and her companion asked if we'd go along and give her family a private sitting. During the sitting that followed, Dennis came through indicating that snow was important – he didn't say why but showed Mike and I a picture of himself standing sideways on. Going by the way he held himself, it looked to me as though he had a problem with his hip or back. Mike had noticed his slightly bent stance too.

His daughter Loraine (the lady who'd invited us to hold the family sitting) explained that her father's wartime bomber was

129

attacked on March 16th 1944 by an ME110. The plane survived the first onslaught but a second burst of fire hit the outer starboard engine which burst into flames. They were given the chance to bail out but since the aeroplane had plenty of altitude to play with, they donned parachutes and persevered with their mission, determined to bomb their target before abandoning their aircraft. A searing cannon and machine-gunfire attack from above by a JU88 put paid to that heroic aim and Dennis was hit in the legs and blasted from his seat across the escape hatch. The cockpit filled with acrid smoke and Dennis couldn't see his comrades. Realising he'd burn to death in moments, he bailed out and found himself tumbling through space with both of his legs blown off below the knee.

After pulling the ripcord, he floated down and landed heavily in the snow where he lay until three young German girls came to his aid and took him to a German infirmary. His luck – if you could call it luck – was that his landing in the snow meant that his stumps had frozen solid. Had they not he would surely have bled to death. In later life, many of the people who knew him didn't realise that his legs were missing because he walked so well! He went on to meet and marry a very special lady called Gladys and brought up a wonderful family with whom we're lucky enough to have become friends through spiritualism.

I feel that we were meant to meet and become friends with this wonderful family. They'd heard about my service on the Carl Chin radio show, on which Dennis had been recounting extracts of his life story. A member of their family had died earlier of cancer and, having heard mention of my service on the very same radio show, they had decided that it was an omen and that they were meant to attend. I'm so pleased that they did – not only because they have all become such good friends but also because Dennis appears from time to time to help me out when I'm on the rostrum. In my opinion he's one of life's unsung heroes and is still doing his best to help people, even from the other side.

One day whilst Tess was at our home with some other friends we were practising giving messages to one another. When it came to Tess's turn she gave a perfect link, including a complete description, cause of death, name and the reason for their visit. The whole message was understood and accepted by the lady, whom Tess had never met before. Tess jumped up and down, punching the air with her fists, shouting, 'Yes! Yes! Yes!'

It was pure excitement. Any medium understands that feeling when you first get it right!

You'd be surprised at the different reactions you get from people when they know you're a medium. I have my hair done regularly by a man called Carl Flavell who owns a hairdressers in Boldmere near where I live. Every time he cuts my hair we wait for him to say something – and he never lets us down! He'll suddenly smile and blush as he says, 'Have you got any gossip then?'

By this, he means messages from the spirit world. This never fails to make us laugh – and he does a good job of my hair at the same time! The spirits usually try to give him some help and encouragement along the way! For instance, they said that he and his wife would have a baby – which they did. They also told him to watch out because they felt that something was wrong with the wiring in his shop and that it could catch fire. He wasn't convinced but a few months later he started to have problems with lights blowing and so on. The place had to be rewired! Needless to say he bore in mind the spirit warning and got it done straight away!

I would like to point out that mediums are not fortune-tellers. It's just that the spirits sometimes give us information about the future to reassure people, warn them of danger or just to make them think and realise that there is no death.

I have a sister called Hazel, whom Mike, the children and I call

'Crazy Hazy'. This is because she has been known to do some very zany things. She and her partner have three children, Mikaela (as I've mentioned before) and twin daughters. Hazel would make a brilliant medium because she has an amazing amount of psychic power – as has her partner. Nevertheless she was surprised and scared by two incidents involving the twins.

The first was when Hazel was at home alone with her baby twins. She had put them to bed upstairs in their separate cots, placed about a foot apart. They were only two months old so, when she heard one of them crying, she checked on them straight away – only to find that they were both fast asleep, cuddled up together in the same cot! Panicked, she phoned me in the hope that I could give her an explanation, which, of course, I could. It was because twins born to two psychic parents seem to be born with a double dose of psychic awareness – which is obviously so in this case.

Another time, when the twins were about six months old, they were playing in their playpen, which had fairly high sides. Hazel went upstairs to the bathroom and when she came down one of them was playing with a teddy bear on the settee on the opposite side of the room. It was impossible for her to climb out. And they had been alone in the house. Yet, once again, she had somehow transported herself out of the playpen! The same twin would always stare at me, smiling as soon as she was old enough, her eyes following me wherever I went. I believe that she could see my guides. There's no other explanation for her fascination with me, especially since I don't get the chance to see them very often because they live in Derby. It's not as if they know me very well.

As I've said before, psychic ability is in the genes. Not only have our children got the ability to communicate with the spirit world but our grand-daughter, Leah, also has the gift. You can always tell by looking at them when they're babies. If they spend a lot of time staring into mid-air and giggling as if they are laughing at someone who isn't there. This is a sign that they have the gift. As soon as Leah was old enough to talk she would chatter away to someone who was invisible to her mum, dad and other onlookers. When she was three years old she told us that his name was Toula and that he wore a dress and a seatbelt! I immediately asked whether he drove a car. Clearly frustrated at this, she flung her arms in the air and said, 'No Nanny, he wears a seatbelt!'

As she said this she motioned with one arm a diagonal movement from her right shoulder to her left hip. We laughed at her impatience with us and concluded that this man in the spirit world must have worn a toga and sash. He was obviously one of her guides. One day, about a month later, we were visiting Dawn, when Leah watched her mum go into the kitchen to make a cup of tea and said, 'Why has that lady followed Mummy into the kitchen?'

Mike and I hadn't been looking as Dawn left the room so we were puzzled. I went to the kitchen to investigate and, sure enough, there was Dawn's grandmother standing behind her left shoulder. I whispered this to Dawn and called Leah – who didn't hear me because there was another room between the kitchen and the lounge, where Leah was busy playing with her grandfather. I fetched her and, once back in the kitchen, asked, 'is the lady here that followed Mummy?'

Yes nanny, there she is, ' came Leah's reply as she pointed behind Dawn's left shoulder.

'Don't say that,' Dawn said with a shiver.

'I would die,' she said, looking at me, 'if she told me that someone was there whom I couldn't see whilst you weren't here to tell me who it was!'

We really laughed at this and I told her that if it ever happened she just had to ask the spirits who's there and they'll tell her! Leah recently celebrated her fourth birthday so, together with her Mum and her friend, Mike and I took her to Weston Super Mare for the day. On the way home in the car, Leah announced, 'I don't talk to Toula any more.'

Why don't you talk to Toula any more darling?' I asked, intrigued.

'Because he keeps hitting me on the head when I don't do things the way he tells me to and I don't like it,' she said, seriously, 'But a new lady talks to me now and she says "If you don't need me to tell you things then that's all right. But if you do need me to that is all right too." She sings this song.'

With that she started singing a song that we'd never heard before. She then asked Dawn's friend to join in. He said that he couldn't because he didn't know the words.

'Well copy her like I am!' she replied. Of course, he replied that he couldn't hear her.

'Of course you can. Listen!' was Leah's impatient response. But he still insisted that he couldn't hear so she said, 'All right, I'll copy her and you can copy me.'

And that's what they did. Fortunately for Leah, this gift will be encouraged and nurtured so, one day, she should grow up to be a very good medium.

One night, whilst Mike and I were asleep in bed, he was woken by the sensation of leathery fingers rubbing across his arm in a scratching motion. He sat up and looked over at me but could see that my arms were elsewhere. He sat upright in bed and the fingers, which belonged to my gorilla from the spirit world, disappeared. The following morning I was quite poorly and told Mike that the gorilla was only trying to let him know that he should look after me. The gorilla's job in the spirit world is to protect me and that's exactly what he was doing. That's why he was so gentle on Mike's arm – careful not to hurt him.

Anyone who wants to develop their mediumship should

remember that they are in charge of their body and brain at all times – so they should only allow Spirit the amount of access that they're happy with. It is also important to accept that strength of mind and connecting with the spirit world are two different things.

For me, things that go bump in the night could never be scary because they're normal for me. I could never be afraid of Izeakial and would be terribly worried if he wasn't on the stairs, alone or in company, when I went to the bathroom at night.

Everyone is psychic to some degree but not everyone can become a medium. You can, however, help your own life and those of people around you to go more smoothly by developing the psychic powers you have. Practice, practice and more practice is the answer. It helped me and I assure you that it will help you.

I wish you all the best of luck on your path to spiritual development. And remember, the thing to keep in your head is:

I can. And I will.

Then, I assure you, you'll have a chance of it happening for you just as it did for me.

Publisher's note: Jean concludes her book with this interesting and illuminating anecdote:

Whilst conducting a service in a Spiritualist Church recently, a young gentleman in his late thirties came through to speak to his mother. He went on to say that he had been bludgeoned around the head and shoulders and had also been stabbed several times. He described blood bubbles coming up his throat and choking him. He told me to tell his mum that he was sorry for all the distress that he had caused her through his life and subsequent death. He was extremely emotional, as you would imagine, and gave information about people involved in his own lifestyle. For obvious reasons I do not wish to divulge all the details, but he did say, "Tell Mum - it is tomorrow and I will be there."

At this point in time his family could not understand what he meant. However, the following morning it was announced on television that two men had been arrested in connection with the murder and would appear in court that morning. This was obviously what he had been trying to tell the family and to reassure them that he would also be there. He wanted his family to know that he was at last at peace and to say, "Mum I love you, and I really am sorry. Do not worry about me, I am okay, and at peace."